IN
THE COMPANY OF
MY SOLITUDE

OTHER PERSEA ANTHOLOGIES

POETS FOR LIFE: SEVENTY-SIX POETS RESPOND TO AIDS
Edited by Michael Klein

PAPER PANCE: 55 LATINO POETS
Edited by Victor Hernández Cruz, Leroy V. Quintana, & Virgil Suarez

IMAGINING AMERICA: STORIES FROM THE PROMISED LAND
Edited by Wesley Brown & Amy Ling

VISIONS OF AMERICA: PERSONAL NARRATIVES FROM THE PROMISED LAND
Edited by Wesley Brown & Amy Ling

AMERICA STREET: A MULTICULTURAL ANTHOLOGY OF STORIES
Edited by Anne Mazer

GOING WHERE I'M COMING FROM: MEMOIRS OF AMERICAN YOUTH
Edited by Anne Mazer

FIRST SIGHTINGS: CONTEMPORARY STORIES OF AMERICAN YOUTH
Edited by John Loughery

INTO THE WIDENING WORLD: INTERNATIONAL COMING-OF-AGE STORIES
Edited by John Loughery

SHOW ME A HERO: GREAT CONTEMPORARY STORIES ABOUT SPORTS
Edited by Jeanne Schinto

IN THE COMPANY OF MY SOLITUDE

AMERICAN WRITING FROM THE AIDS PANDEMIC

Edited by Marie Howe and Michael Klein

PERSEA BOOKS
NEW YORK

Requests for permission to reprint or for any information should be
addressed to the publisher:
PERSEA BOOKS, INC.
60 Madison Avenue
New York, New York 10010

Library of Congress Cataloging-in-Publication Data

In the company of my solitude : American writing from the AIDS
pandemic / edited by Marie Howe and Michael Klein.
p.   cm.
Includes bibliographical references.
ISBN 0-89255-208-5
1. AIDS (Disease)   I. Howe, Marie, 1950– .   II. Klein, Michael,
1954 Aug. 17–
RC607.A26I52   1995   94-47983
362.1'969792–dc20   CIP

Designed by REM Studio, Inc.
Set in Berthold Garamond by Keystrokes, Lenox, Massachusetts
Printed and bound by Haddon Craftsmen, Scranton, Pennsylvania
Cover printed by Lynn Art, New York, New York

First Edition

"*There are hawks along the highway to Rhode Island. Now and again I drive the hour to see them. I keep a steady pace through the flat bogland, past the low-reaching pines. . . . There are angels in the company of my solitude. They wave mahogany tresses, braids that fall like the cool balm of silk. They kiss my red wrinkled skin. We walk together in the park, sit quietly by the water. They remember my beauty. I catch it in their eyes in a certain gray light . . . .*"

—JAMES ASSATLY

CONTENTS

CONTENTS

INTRODUCTION

Michael Klein

It's the lion preface of March and I am listening to Piano
Concerto No. 1 by Franz Liszt in Provincetown, Massachusetts,
where a winter storm has arrived rather quietly–the way AIDS
arrived in the media in 1980–81. Snow must have lost its way
coming through here. There's a huge wind with traces of rain in
it, but the gray day has made it look like the storm is over rather
than only just beginning–or are we in the middle of it?

Here it comes, the gorgeous, restrained, but anticipatory
piano solo in the concerto, and still no snow–just more of the
same gray wind shuddering in the trees. I think of AIDS in the
same way I think of this storm–that it, too, has either just
begun, or it's over, or we're in the middle of it. Well, everyone
knows it's not over. We are in the fifteenth year of AIDS in
America. How is this possible?

When Michael Braziller of Persea Books asked me to edit
this anthology, my immediate thought was, I can't. I can't read
another word about AIDS. I had edited the book *Poets for Life*,
and while that reading and writing experience had been a turning point in my life, I just didn't think I could bear reading
more testimony in this particular historical transcript. But I also
knew that this subject calls me the way a place calls me, and I

have to go–like Provincetown, for instance, where I live from time to time in order to allow certain aspects of my being to come through, to breathe the air that Mark Doty has said "is the air of people's lives changing"–I had to go to AIDS writing.

In that spirit, then, of knowing the changing world and living with those changes, I came to this second anthology. But I would edit it only if I could do so with Marie Howe, whose poems about her brother John's death from AIDS had moved me so much and had started our great friendship.

Marie and I wanted to put together a book of writing about AIDS that would interpret this particular time and acknowledge the progressive realization that the effects of this pandemic are more far-reaching than we had ever imagined. AIDS has changed the world. This is a book of changes.

And we wanted to collect writing that was smart, funny, reflective, angry, and immediate–not necessarily from people who were writers by profession, but from people who felt, maybe for the first time, an urgency to "get it down on paper." We wrote to everyone we knew and networked mostly on the telephone. We were especially interested in work from people who haven't been heard from–voices from the homeless shelter, the high school, the sex-worker industry. And it was in the act of getting this particular material that Marie and I were most moved–because AIDS as subject matter had enabled previously non-writers to write.

I'd like to dedicate this work and gathering of such passionate and varied voices to the memory of Melvin Dixon, who died in 1992. The last time I saw Melvin alive was at the Out/Write conference of that same year. He had just given what has now become a legendary closing address (included here), but it was something else even then, while he was living with it, and it was precisely his living with it that made us listen on the edges of our seats.

It was very much with Melvin in mind and the great thought offered by him, that the dead can be listening for their names, that Marie and I decided to edit this book. There's something Whitmanesque *(look for me under your bootsoles)* about this kind of wanting to be remembered (well, not just remembered but actually recalled). Melvin's life, at the end, was about making sure that the world he loved so vitally and dearly was not left with an empty space his body had been in, but with the fullness of what his living and writing did.

INTRODUCTION

Marie Howe

I didn't want to write this introduction: the book isn't finished, the man who . . . the woman who might . . . that high school kid who would have. . . . Who wouldn't have an overwhelming desire to make a few more phone calls? The voices line up like luminous people moving constantly to the back of a crowded bus, and they disappear out the back door that keeps swinging open at the stops.

And the voices that never get written down or recorded? And the people who don't have entry to the world that copies and publishes? Or the people who died before they could write what they wanted to say? Or who chose to keep their health status private or secret? My own brother, John Howe, made us promise not to tell anyone he was infected with the AIDS virus. "Tell everyone after I'm dead," he said. "Tell everyone then."

How do you anthologize silence? It's here too: between the turning pages.

And this: The last time I had dinner with my brother John at a restaurant he took my two hands in his hands and held them across the white tablecloth. "I'm going to die soon," he said, "I want you to know that." And I said, "I think I do know." And he said, "I know I'm going to die soon. . . . What surprises me is that you don't." "But I do know," I said. He said, "Know what?" and I said, "Know that you're going to die," and he said, "No, I'm surprised that you don't know that *you* are."

The plight of people living with AIDS is our plight, amplified: living and dying at the same time. And they know all too well that we're all living and dying in a culture agonizing over notions of sexuality, race, class, religion, gender, health care, housing, who's a legal family, who gets buried where. . . .

"Is There a Future?" Mark Doty asks. Paul Monette's dog begins to bark at people when they *leave* the house. Deborah Salazar tells us "The Bad News Is the Bad News Is the Same." We need to listen to what these people have to say.

"What's next?" I asked John after another MRI, and he said, smiling through the phone, "What's next for me is a plate of blueberry pancakes. What's next for you?" He was right, of course. The future might be now. Or, as he used to say with a maddening, reassuring frequency, "This is what you have been waiting for." And I'd say "What?" And he said "This," a sort of looking around.

This book is for my brother John who lived and died with AIDS. And for all of us: you and me; then and now or later or soon.

IN
THE COMPANY OF
MY SOLITUDE

IS THERE A
FUTURE?

Mark Doty

Mark Doty's *My Alexandria* (University of Illinois Press, 1993) was chosen for the National Poetry Series by Philip Levine, received the *Los Angeles Times* Book Award, was a finalist for the National Book Award, and won the National Book Critics Circle Award. His partner of twelve years, Wally Roberts, died in January 1994.

In 1989, not long after my partner Wally and I took the HIV test, the pain in my back—which had been a kind of chronic, low-level problem—became acute. I went to a chiropractor I'd seen before, a rough-and-tumble kind of guy with a strange, cluttered little office on a shady part of Main Street in the Vermont town where we lived then. Dr. Crack, as I thought of him, was his own secretary, and furnished his office with all manner of cast-offs and inspirational posters, along with many implements of vague and mysterious use. In general, he did not inspire confidence. He snapped me around with considerable force, and though I felt much better after being treated by him, I also felt a mounting sense of nervousness about the degree of force he used. One day the crack my neck made as he whipped it into place was so loud that I resolved to see the New Age doctor my friends had spoken so highly of. She had cured one friend of a nervous tic in the eye simply by manipulating a spot on her spine; others swore by her gentler style of manipulation. On my first visit, as I lay on my stomach in a room full of ferns and charts marking the locations of chakras and pressure points, she touched one vertebra which throbbed, seemed almost to ring, painfully, like a struck tuning fork. I felt she'd touched the very center of the pain in my sacrum, the weak spot where my ache originated. When I told her this, she said that the particular vertebra she was touching represented "faith in the future." Under her tentative touches—delivered with less pressure than one would use to push an elevator button—my back simply got worse, but her diagnosis was so penetratingly accurate that I never forgot it. After a while I went back to Dr. Crack, and my back got better but not the rupture in my faith.

The test results had come back negative for me, positive for Wally, but it didn't seem to matter so much which of us carried the antibodies for the virus. We'd been together eight years; we'd surrounded ourselves with a house and animals and garden, tokens of permanency; our continuance was somehow assumed, an essential aspect of living that made life what it was. That we would continue to be, and to be together, had about it the unquestioned nature of a given, the tacit starting point from which the rest of our living proceeded. The news was as devastating as if I'd been told I was positive myself. In retrospect, I think of two different metaphors for the way it affected me.

The virus seemed to me, first, like a kind of solvent which dissolved the future, our future, a little at a time. It was like a dark stain, a floating, inky transparency hovering over Wally's body, and its intention was to erase the time ahead of us, to make that time, each day, a little smaller.

And then I thought of us as standing on a kind of sandbar, the present a narrow strip of land which had previously seemed enormous, without any clear limits. Oh, there was a limit out there, somewhere, of course, but not anywhere in sight. But the virus was a kind of violent chill current, one which was eroding, at who knew what speed, the ground upon which we stood. If you watched, you could see the edges crumbling.

Four years have passed. For two of them, we've lived with the knowledge of Wally's immune status, though he was blessedly asymptomatic; for the last two years, we have lived with AIDS. His has not been the now-typical pattern of dizzying descents into opportunistic infections followed by recoveries. Instead, he's suffered a gradual, steady decline, an increasing weakness which, a few months ago, took a sharp turn for the worse. He is more or less confined to bed now, with a few forays up and out in his wheelchair; he is physically quite weak, though alert and present, and every day I am grateful he's with me, though I will admit that I also rail and struggle against the limitations his health places upon us. As he is less capable, less present, I do battle with my own sense of loss at the same time as I try not to let the present disappear under the grief of those disappearances and the anticipatory grief of a future disappearance.

And I struggle as well with the way the last four years have forced me to rethink my sense of the nature of the future.

I no longer think of AIDS as a solvent but perhaps rather as a kind of intensifier, something which makes things more what they already are. AIDS changes the degree of things, but not the things themselves. I learned this from watching Wally change, and watching changes in the lives of friends who were either ill themselves or giving care to those who were. They simply became more themselves: more generous or terrified, more cranky or afraid, more doubtful or more trusting. As individual and unpredictable as this illness seems to be, the one thing I found I could say with certainty was this: AIDS makes things more intensely what they already are. Eventually I understood that this truism then must apply to me as well, and of course it applied to my anxiety about the future.

Because the truth was I'd *never* really believed in a future, always had trouble imagining ongoingness, continuance, a place in the unfolding chain of things. I was raised on apocalypse. My Christian grandmother—whose Tennessee fundamentalism reduced not a jot her generosity or spiritual grace—used to read me passages from the Book of Revelation and talk about the imminence of the Last Days; the hymns we sang figured this world as a veil of appearances, and sermons in church characterized the human world as a flimsy screen behind which the world's real actors enacted the struggles and dramas of a loftier realm. Not struggles, exactly, since the outcome was foreknown, the lake of fire and the fiery pit, the eternal chorus of the saved, but dramatic in the sense of scale, or scope, of how large and mighty the music of our salvation was.

By the time I was an adolescent I was quickly outgrowing religion when another sense of the apocalyptic replaced it, the late sixties' faith in the imminence of revolution, a belief that was not without its own religious tinge and implication. Everything promised that the world could not stay the same; the foundations of order were quavering, both the orders of the social arena and of consciousness itself. When the Hog Farm commune came to my town in their schoolbus painted Day-glo Tibetan, the people who came tumbling out into the park had about them the aura of a new world, one where we'd see things more clearly, with the doors of perception cleansed; new vision would yield new harmony, transformation. I couldn't articulate much about the nature of the future I felt was in the offing, but I was certain that certain sorts of preparation seemed ridiculously beside the point. Imagine buying, say, life insurance, or investing in a retirement plan, when the world as we'd always known it was burning?

One sort of apocalyptic scenario has replaced another: endings ecological or nuclear, scenarios of depleted ozone or global starvation or, finally, epidemic. All my life I've lived with a future which constantly diminishes but never vanishes.

Apocalypse is played out now in a personal scale; it is not in the sky above us but in our bed.

In the sort of museums we used to visit on family vacations when I was a kid, I used to love those rooms which displayed collections of minerals in a kind of closet or chamber which would, at the push of a button, darken. Then ultraviolet lights would begin to glow and the minerals would seem to come alive: new colors, new possibilities and architectures revealed. Plain stones became fantastic, "futuristic"—a strange word which suggests, accurately, that these colors had something of the world-to-come about them. Of course there wasn't any black light in the center of the earth, in the caves where they were quarried; how strange that these stones should have to be brought here, bathed in this unnatural light in order for their transcendent characters to emerge. Irradiation revealed a secret aspect of the world. Imagine illness as that light: demanding, torturous, punitive, it nonetheless reveals more of what things are. A certain glow of being appears. I think this is what is meant when we speculate that death is what makes love possible. Not that things need to be able to die in order for us to love them, but that things need to die in order for us to know *what they are.* Could we really know anything that wasn't transient, not becoming more itself in the strange, unearthly light of dying? The button pushed, the stones shine, all mystery and beauty, implacable, fierce, austere.

Will there be a moment when you will die to me?

Of course you will cease to breathe, sometime; probably you will cease to breathe before I do, though there's no way to know this, really. But your being, your being-in-me, that will last as long as I do, won't it? There's a poem of Tess Gallagher's about the aftermath of her husband's death, one called "Now That I Am Never Alone." Of course.

Is my future, then, remembering you? Inscribing the name, carrying the memory, being remembered as one who remembered. The work of the living is remembering, and the collective project of memory is enormous; it involves the weight of all our dead, the ones we have known ourselves and the ones we know only from stories. It is necessary to recall not just names but also faces, stories, incidents, gestures, tics, nuances, those particular human attributes that distinguish us as individuals. A name, after all, emptied of contexts, is only a name. But a name is better than nothing. Lists of names, like the ones read at ceremonies around the Quilt, remind us of enormity, scale, the legions of the dead. Details, stories, remind us of the particular loved body and being of X and Y or—say it—W.

Even photos, after a while, lend themselves to speculation but don't say much. When I was a child we had a big metal fruitcake tin, the kind printed with golden trellises and scrolls, full of family photos. Many of them were inherited, and even though there were names penned on the back—Alice, Lavinia, Mary—over time an increasing number of them went unrecognized, those who remembered them gone. Although we had names for them, and faces, they had lost their particular humanness when we no longer had their stories.

Let this, then, be one more inscription, one version of Wally's and my story. We have been together eleven years, fused in a partnership that felt, after a while, elemental, like bedrock. If I write about it as if it's already done, that's because so much of it *is*— W. is less present, spends almost weekly more time alseep, and is less and less capable of involvement in the stuff of mutual life. We're pushed into a different kind of relation. (Those sentences were true when I wrote them, but this week he's much more alert—still unable to walk but ready to get out of the house, ready to shop for new shoes and magazines.

It's only Wednesday and this week we have already been out three times, me pushing the wheelchair to town, to restaurants where we can sit outside, along the rough street and rougher sidewalk. We are laughing a lot, full of the pleasures of reprieve. Nothing about who we are together has changed. We have a present again.)

"Look, I'm living," Rilke writes in the *Duino Elegies*. "On what? Neither my childhood nor my future is growing smaller." Like most great poems, I guess, this is both true and not true. Certainly the past is accomplished, complete; what has been is over and nothing can change it now, nothing can change except our perspectives, the way we interpret or understand. And the future *is* infinite, if not our personal fates then that great flux of matter and spirit which goes on, in which we will in some way participate—as energy if not as individuals.

But at the same time the past *feels* diminished when the future seems to shrink. Mourning contracts the eye like a camera lens in strong light; the aperture of the soul shrinks to a tiny pinpoint which admits only grief. When I am overcome—as I am, about once a week—by the prospect of losing my lover, I can't see any kind of ongoingness; my vision becomes one-pointed, like looking through the wrong end of a telescope, and the world seems smaller and further away and sad, a difficult place which no one would much want to inhabit.

The grief which sweeps over me is the grief of anticipation; it isn't like that which must be experienced by the surviving lovers and family of someone who's died. It is a grief in expectation of grief, and it carries with it a certain degree of guilt, since one feels that what one really *should* be doing is enjoying the moment, being together *now* while it is possible to do so rather than giving in to some gloomy sense of incipient loss. And while most of the time I can maintain that sensibility—the preciousness of the present, the importance of not projecting too far ahead, not trying to feel my way blindly toward the future—I can't sustain it all the time. The future's an absence, a dark space up ahead like the socket of a pulled tooth. And like that gap, I can't quite stay away from it, hard as I may try. The space opened up in the future insists on being filled with *something:* attention, tears, imagination, longing.

The more one tries to live in the present, it seems, the more one learns the inseparability of time, the artifice of our construction of the trinity of experience: yesterday, today, tomorrow meld into one another, blur in and out. We move among them at the speed of memory or of anticipation. Trying to remain in the moment is like living in three dimensions, in sheerly physical space; the mind doesn't seem to be whole unless it also occupies the dimension of time, which grants to things their depth and complexity, the inherent dignity and drama of their histories, the tragedy of their possibilities. What then does it mean, can it mean, to "be here now"? That discipline of paying attention to things-as-they-are in the present seems simply to reveal the way the nature of each thing is anchored to time's passage, cannot exist outside of time.

Take, for instance, the salt marsh where I walked, the day that I began to write this essay in my head, near Wood End Light, out beyond Herring Cove Beach at the end of Cape Cod, where I live. That marsh is perhaps my favorite place in the world; it feels inexhaustible to me, in all the contradictions which it yokes so gracefully in its own being. It is both austere and lush, wet and dry, constant and ceaselessly changing, secretive and open. I have never, in years of walks, grown weary of looking at it, perhaps because there is no single thing which constitutes "it"; the marsh is a whole shifting confluence of aspects. At low tide it's entirely dry, a Sahara of patterned sand and the tough green knots of sea lavender, beach grass around the edges of the beds of the tidal rivers gleaming, where it bends and catches light along the straps of its leaves. As the tide mounts, twice a day, this desert disappears beneath the flood. It is a continuous apocalpyse; Sahara becomes sea becomes sand again, in a theater of furious mutability.

Its lesson—or at least the lesson I draw from it today, since this teacher's so vast and has so many sorts of possibilities hidden in its repertoire—is that what one can *see* is the present, the dimension of landscape which is in front of us now, but now is shaped by the past, backed by it, as it were, the way the glass of a mirror's backed by silver; it's what lies behind the present that gives it color and sheen. And now is always giving way, always becoming, and it is this progress into the future which gives things the dynamic dimension of forwardness they could not have were they composed solely of a past and a present. If past and present are the glass and its silver backing, then future is what is coming-to-be in the mirror, the image that presents itself, intrudes into the frame. I mix my metaphors with abandon, because I am talking near the edge of the unsayable, at the difficult intersection of what I can feel but barely say.

Wally is in my body; my body is in this text; this text is light on my computer screen, electronic impulse, soon to be print, soon to be in the reader's body, yours—remembered or forgotten, picked up or set aside, it nonetheless acquires a strange kind of physical permanence, a persistence. My friend Billy, hearing about this essay, says "long-term survivors, you've got to address long-term survivors." It's a message of hope he wants; hope is perhaps simply a stance towards the world, finally, a stance of participation, or inseparability. That which cannot be separated cannot perish. The world has one long-term survivor, which is the world.

This is how I see through the wider end of the telescope, when my perspective on the world is wide enough to see us as part of this vast interchange of being, not its center. On other days, the water of grief—deep, impenetrable, dark, cold water—pours over everything and I am lightless, unseeing.

Whether or not I have faith in the future, whether there is a personal future for Wally or whether I am all there'll be of us, and then those who will read or remember me later all there'll be of me—well, whatever I believe today, whatever my marsh and my study convince me of, the future does go on without us. The world doesn't need us to continue, although it does need us to attend, to study, to name. We are two elements of the world's consciousness of itself, and thus we are necessary, replaceable and irreplaceable at once. Someone will take our places, but then again there will never be anyone like us, no one who will see quite this way; we are a sudden flowering of seeing, among the millions of such blossomings. Like the innumerable tiny stars on the branching stalk of the sea lavender; it takes how many, a thousand, to construct this violet sheen, this little shaking cloud of flowers?

Eternity, Blake said, is in love with the productions of time. Perhaps in fact eternity inheres in the things that time makes; perhaps that's all of eternity we'll know: the wave, the flower, the repeated endless glimmerings and departures of tides.

My error, which perhaps really *does* express itself in that pain in the fifth vertebra, lies in thinking the future's something we can believe or disbelieve, trust or doubt. It's the element we breathe. Our position in time—ungraspable thing!—is the element in which we move. Our apocalypse is daily, but so is our persistence.

THE BAD NEWS
IS THE BAD NEWS
IS THE SAME

Deborah Salazar

Deborah Salazar was born in Ecuador but lived for much of her life as an illegal alien in the United States. In 1988, she received her MFA from Louisiana State University and was granted permanent U.S. residency. Her poems, essays, stories, and translations have been widely published. She lives in Baton Rouge, Louisiana.

David and I used to joke about going to New York whenever AIDS finally wipes out the old-guard art world and *taking over*. He was going to be the finest, longest-lashed Delta darling the paparazzi ever chased; I was going to determine the literary tastes of the twenty-second century. So it's not like we weren't prepared for the pandemic. "If it's spread by kissing, we're *all* dead," David used to say. We'd both become sexually active, within our respective orientations, shortly after high school in-the-seventies-when-no-one-knew-any-better, but by the early eighties, after all the *Donahue*s, his fag friends were all using condoms, and my girlfriends were definitely feeling more morning-after anxiety. So it's not like we didn't expect AIDS to touch our languorous, hot-hormoned south Louisiana lives eventually. But we didn't expect it to knock the door down; by

1990, three of my friends, guys I'd known since grade school, were (this is south Louisiana and even PC types don't avoid gentle euphemisms) "sick."

David was the first to be diagnosed. It was World AIDS Awareness Day, December 1, 1990, and the television in the ceiling corner of his hospital room was running constant newspieces about AIDS. David first asked his mother to leave and then said, starting to cry, "It *is* AIDS." I took his hand and started to talk words I don't remember; all I remember is at every pause in my speech, there was this matter-of-fact reporter's voice speaking phrases like "high-risk group," "gay and lesbian community," and "an estimated one million infected people in the U.S."

Not too long ago, I saw a piece in *Spy* magazine called "The Good News Is the Bad News Is the Same": it showed *The New York Times* reporting the same "estimated one million infected" line in 1985, 1988, 1990, and 1992. I went berserk: Does *anybody* have a clue to knowing how many of us are going to die? The press has it that one out of every 170 people in my home state is infected with HIV—that's a little worse than the national average. Leaving out old people and children, that puts it too close for comfort in my own sexually active age group. Draw the circumference tighter, say around the bisexual arty community, and I start to get a hint of what AIDS means to my generation; it defines our living by forecasting our peculiar way of dying. Go talk about *that* on David Letterman, you facetious twenty-nothing generation sex puppies, I thought. For all the suicidal musings of my yearning, extended adolescence, I at last get to confront this sort of mortality: my generation truly believes it is going to die young.

David promised he would haunt me. He said he would terrorize my dog and empty all my perfume bottles. It's a Scorpio-Pisces thing, I agreed. If anyone could tune in with him after death, it would have to be me. Because when we were kids, the two of us made the ouija board squeal; our joined psychic stuff soared over it with glee.

A week before his death, I reminded him of his promise. He was making grabbing gestures at my face from his hospital bed. We'd been through our goodbyes before, lots of times, every time one of the doctors said this might be it, for two years and five hospitalizations now, and I was running out of things to say. Maybe David had too; an infection had reached his brain and he'd lost his speech. He was strapped to his bed by the elbows, so he couldn't pull out his oxygen and I.V. tubes. He grabbed at my face a couple times and then caught the hand I held up and squeezed it; meanwhile his mother and sister started to ooh and aah and to exclaim, "Look at that! Look at that!" We all knew he knew who I was. It was a high moment, because he had recognized someone. "David, David," I said. "I love you so much. Will you come visit me? After–?"

"Yes," he said. And his free hand made this tossing gesture, like "go on" or "get out of here," and I swear that before he closed his eyes to sleep again, they made some melodramatic, hyper-sarcastic roll to the ceiling. Like, "Oh please. These good-byes are getting tedious." That's what he would have said, I think.

David died exactly two years to the day of his diagnosis, on World AIDS Awareness Day, 1992. Right on schedule–three out of four PWAs die within two years of being diagnosed, or at least so say the pamphlets they hand out at the hospital. But I counted on David's living longer than most, maybe living until the cure is discovered. He got better at first. He gained weight. He looked like everybody else–better than most, actually. Tall and twenty-eight, *GQ* handsomeness in an Armani sweater. One night we went dancing, and it struck me: not one of the pretty young people whirling around in here knows how he or she is going to die. It's like the anxiety of *how* is making them dance–what symptom is going to come first? KS, sudden dementia, a persistent cough? Or will it be snakebite, a car crash, a falling brick? I comforted myself for a while with the idea that "everyone is born dying." But I was such a virgin—not only to AIDS but to death itself. Sure, I'd known people who'd died, but no one I *loved*.

What did *I* know about slow, painful death except what I saw in movies that made me cry? *Terms of Endearment,* etc. . . . But you don't cry when you're watching a slow, painful AIDS death in real time; you deal with whatever needs to be dealt with then and there. At first, everyone is embarrassed. There's an urgent awareness of, yes, *sex* that needs to be acknowledged by the sick person and everyone around him. Imagine a PWA (if he or she is not a hemophiliac or a child or a pursey virgin who's only ever opened her mouth for her dentist) having to face parents dealing with the plain fact that their child has had sex. David's parents knew for certain he was gay, but there were still whole corridors of closets he hadn't come out of, as far as Mama and Daddy were concerned. The day after the diagnosis, his father was musing with me in the hospital waiting room, "No, I don't think David ever fooled with ——. Who else could he have got it from?" I was sitting there, talking with a genteel Southern gentleman about his son's gay sex life. I was thrilled and humiliated, shocked into a sweet, weird social situation I'd only ever imagined existing in pockets of utopia somewhere in San Francisco. After David's funeral, all the tall handsome gay pallbearers and some of the younger mourners went out to eat oysters and drink beer, away from our parents who were look-ing at us with some new awareness and grief (knowing that your parents are worrying about your sex life is just too much after a funeral). We went to one of those restaurant-bars where a lot of our generation spend hours after school or work, and there we were, babies born during the Pill-era, with our Who-is-Betty-Friedan and Does-Sandra-lick-Madonna mentalities, with our eating-disordered torsos dressed to kill, there we were, more nervous than anything else about *sex,* and here was the phenomenon of AIDS pushing that anxiety to the breaking point.

You deal with whatever needs to be dealt with then and there. You adjust I.V. tubes so they don't bend, you pass the vomit bucket, you sit in the hospital room and watch endless television, you listen to the medical machinery bleep and whir, and you answer the phone every time it rings and say "No change." Even after the death happens, the bad news is that the bad news is still the same. It's only been a few months since David's died, and in that time celebrities have died from AIDS, about one every two weeks, Peter Allen, the Brady dad, Nureyev, Tony Perkins, Arthur Ashe, but I'm still waiting for something to happen, for some wisdom to emerge, for some revelation to shake the world. And I'm still waiting for David to haunt me. Imagine waiting for all these things while waiting for friends to die. You never know who's next. It's like it was all those days in David's hospital room; you expect to learn a kind of saintlike patience, but you never do. You just *are* patient while you're waiting to learn.

LETTER
FROM STEPHEN

Joshua Clover

Joshua Clover writes, "It is *not* important that I in particular wrote the essay. I would request that the piece be published anonymously, except that this would deem to reify further the perception of AIDS as the epidemic which dare not speak its name. My contribution was written only out of love for a man, and because not to write it would have been to give in to grief; in the end, love and not giving in to grief are common ground."

One day I drove 3 hours to see a movie, and then 3 hours home. I find it reassuring that I *could* figure out what day it was if I wanted, because it was the opening of Spike Lee's *Malcolm X*. But when I go over this in my head I never get to the date, the name of the moment.

I got home at about 4 in the morning, undressed and got in bed, the better to enjoy the day's mail: a magazine, letter from Stephen, student loan default notice.

Since Stephen spent a year in Central America while his novel was being published, I mostly call him Esteban with a bogus "Barthelona" lisp. Even if I explained that this is funny because he's from Iowa, child of dangerous and void

Christians, it wouldn't make that much sense. The first couple of pages of his letter—one sheet, front and back—told the story of shoplifting hijinx: clothes, food, books. One run-in at some mall with the Des Moines police, who are as grotesquely pleasant as QuikTrip mini-mart cashiers.

The topic changed on page 3. This is the best sentence: *What I lose in peace of mind, I gain in credibility at* ACT-UP *meetings.* I want to save that sentence in my head, and on this paper. The instant of finding out is explosive—frightening & nauseating—it's the moment the camera lingers on, knowing that everything preceding is suddenly sepia-toned. Now there is a Before and an After.

Much more, I want to save the 2 pages of his letter that came before the small caps of HIV+—the pages when he knew and I didn't and he kept it that way. Because Stephen is a writer, and that's what fierce writers do: they love the story—and thus their reader, naked and lonely in bed at 4 AM—more than their own sorrow. I could say that was life-affirming, if I thought talking that way was anything but a dress-up game for pathos brokers. Those 2 pages made a place which was neither in the nostalgic Before or the heroic-melancholy After.

Of course I would like to live in that place with Stephen forever. And of course that's a lie—really, who would settle for some absolute suspension, some cryogenized fantasy? And of course I have no right to speak of fictional forevers. There is, apparently, a real now, and a lot of reading to be done. We made friends talking about books in a gym in Iowa. I'm using that sheet, pages 1 and 2, as a bookmark. I am thinking about burning buildings down, which we both agree is as politically desirable as it is beautiful. In his most recent letter he talks of shoplifting megadoses of vitamins, which is after all only a small change— God, I'm told, is in the details.

A I D S
A N D   T H E   P O E T R Y
O F   H E A L I N G

Rafael Campo

Rafael Campo is a graduate of Amherst College and Harvard Medical School and currently a resident in Primary Care/Internal Medicine at the University of California, San Francisco. His poetry and essays have appeared in *The Kenyon Review, The Paris Review,* and *Ploughshares.* His first book of poems, *The Other Man Was Me,* was a 1993 National Poetry Series winner.

> *Now you were tired, and yet not tired enough—*
> *Still hungry for the great world you were losing*
> *Steadily in no season of your choosing—*
> *And when at last the whole death was assured,*
> *Drugs having failed, and when you had endured*
> *Two weeks of an abominable constraint,*
> *You faced it equably, without complaint,*
> *Unwhimpering, but not at peace with it.*
> *You'd lived as if your time was infinite.*

FROM *"Lament,"* BY THOM GUNN

The coughing fits continued to worsen until by three in the morning he was doubled over on himself, sweating copiously, almost unable to talk. He likened the pain in his right flank to a hot knife. An invisible torturer stood beside his bed, silent, red-eyed, and mechanical, as tall and malevolent perhaps as one of the digital infusion pumps by which he was receiving intra-venous medication. I rubbed my eyes as I hovered above the bed myself, listening to his lungs, listening to his story of the pain: when it came on, what made it better, what made it worse, how much blood in the sputum and for how long. In between gasps for air, he labored to talk about his hometown of New Orleans and other fantastic places he had been to, what in life had made him happy, what had made him sad, the blood he had once seen on the pavement at an ACT UP demonstration. Then he read me a poem a friend of his had written for him, and by the time he was done, for a few moments the coughing ceased.

I ordered a chest X-ray, trying to feel some of the magical power of being able to see into another person's body. Or maybe the feeling of doing something, anything at all was what I sought. I could hear him start coughing again in his room across the hallway as I wrote, sitting in a comfortable chair in the doctors' lounge, my assessment in his chart. Hemoptysis, fever, pneumothorax, pulmonary embolism, tuberculosis, pneumocys-tis, Kaposi's sarcoma. Not a word about his New Orleans, his wry self-description ("I'm as delicate as a hot-house flower"), the angry demonstrations he had attended; nothing about his race or sexual orientation or the clot-red roses wilting on the bedside table. No mention of the invisible torturer, either, or why he was dying. In short, no mention of us. The story of this pain belongs to all of us, I realized as one-handedly I snapped shut the chart.

When I was in elementary school, newly returned from liv-ing in Venezuela for a few years, a bunch of my new classmates in suburban New Jersey beat me up, calling me "faggot" or "spic," I cannot remember which. That was the first time I saw blood come from my own mouth, red like anger and shame, hot like strangely salty vocal tears. Some other relevant facts are these: I experimented with drugs in high school, but I was afraid of the needles. I was experimenting with sex before high school, but I was afraid of the older boys. I wrote poems secretly, hiding my notebooks in my closet. I thought about killing myself, because those poems knew that I was gay. I graduated at the top of my class, and went on to Amherst College. I fell in love after a trip to New Orleans, where I made love to a Puerto Rican man in a hotel room beneath a handprint on the ceiling. I planned a career in medicine, spending a year off doing basic science research on the AIDS virus. I quit, partly because my job involved killing far too many albino lab rats and "harvesting" their eyes, and partly because I could not see the point of all that pressure to obtain positive results simply to advance one's reputation or find a money-making drug. Eventually I finished medical school, instead of doing graduate work in English, because I hoped to work directly with AIDS patients; the epidemic already had taken root. As a third-year student on the wards, I stuck myself with a needle during my Medicine rotation. When I came down with a fever and cough two weeks later, I thought for the first time, and the millionth time, that I might have AIDS myself. A year later, I wrote a poem about the man whose blood I was drawing at the time, who died of AIDS because there still is no cure. I went to Roxbury, Massachusetts as part of a community health center outreach program, my heart pounding as we distributed condoms to teenagers over threats from adult passersby. Last night, after a chest X-ray was taken of my patient from New Orleans–which revealed nothing–he died before I could tell him any of this, before I could say that in some deeply unspeakable and complicated way that I loved him.

Like my patient's symptoms, I know these bits of my life are related; I want to provide a complete, honest, detailed history, the kind of history I expected from him when he came to the Emergency Room. Then, I want to assemble the information obtained under a single, unifying diagnosis. Except in the end I lack a specific disease, or the name for one. I want to say AIDS, or high-risk group, or empathy, or queer, or Latino, or "it hurts here." I want to say "Dr. Campo, heal me." I want to take an X-ray of myself, and to see not just the bones I will leave behind someday, but directly into my ghostly soul. Or write a poem that miraculously cures AIDS in every language, every culture.

Instead, day in and day out I draw more blood, and then write fragments of iambic pentameter that are incomprehensible to me when I return home late from the hospital—though their rhythms alone, at times, might lull me to sleep. Oftentimes I cannot seem to find a decent vein, or the right words, so I stab blindly. More pain in that. The patients insist that it does not hurt, always giving more, always wanting to be understood. And yet I am speechless, my tube is empty. I have nightmares sometimes that I am drowning in blood, that blood is too plentiful, that there is so much blood I can sink a bucket into it, blood flowing like rich satin sheets rolling in the wind, blood that tastes sweet instead of salty, blood pouring from my mouth like a mournful Spanish song, the blood of my ancestors telling its most precious and guarded secrets, how much potassium, how much sodium, the composition like that of minerals in Cuban soil. Sometimes the blood is an ocean, and the virus is floating on the surface, visible, like a tiny sailboat, or a child's discarded plaything—or is it flying, like an errant seagull? It seems both friendly and ominous, implying that I am close to land. It wants to conquer me brutally, or to bring me gently into a larger world, I am not sure which. Then I awaken, shaking, and check the sheets again to see if they are damp.

I used to think that identity was like immunity. In some ways I still do. If only I could define myself, I think, I would be safe. I would have a secure perimeter I could defend. A territory, a turf, impenetrable even to a virus that pretends to belong to me, even a virus that does belong to me. I would be like Cuba, proclaiming myself AIDS-free, an island, my own world, with set boundaries and yet unexplored interior mountains and jungles. A whole geography of its own to learn. I would be protected from outside influence, from the wars, diseases, and societal upheaval of other peoples. My revolution being completed, the color of blood on my flag would have new, unexpected meanings.

No matter how much I fortify, however, AIDS seems to demand that I suffer too. It claims me. It is insistently part of my identity. At the very least, the pointed finger of epidemiology has singled me out. For once, I fit into too many categories. If money does talk, then its conversations about AIDS have been busy awkwardly naming those of us who are most likely to get the disease. The powerful have been practicing saying out loud, if only briefly, those unmentionable people who are then otherwise ignored and remain oppressed, people who live what seem unimaginable lives: the drug addict we look away from as we pass her in the street, the son who has been disowned and kicked out of his home by his parents, the crack baby abandoned quivering in the incubator. We have said, with our newfangled antiretroviral vocabulary, that AIDS belongs to another people. Medicine for years said AIDS was a gay disease. Government waited several more years before a President said AIDS in public. Religion still implies AIDS is a punishment, meted out by an unloving, unforgiving, and unimaginable God, intent with wrath.

So I am grateful for the poetry that is written about AIDS, in that it has helped me so generously to locate myself in a world irrevocably altered by the presence of the virus. In contrast, the place where I went first for guidance—my medical education—at times steered me away from dealing with AIDS, even working with AIDS patients. Harvard Medical School seemed better designed for attracting money for AIDS research than for preparing its students to care for people with AIDS. Most of the time, it seemed a process invested in reassuring itself that nothing had changed for the greater part of the world. I was taught early on how to be suspicious and how to inflict pain. I was shown slide after slide of schematic representations of the virus infecting nameless, faceless, unidentifiable cells. I was taught universal precautions, by the practice of which I was led to imagine that the universe could be saved from what could only be understood as a grave threat to its, and my profession's, safety. I was armed with toxic drugs, because there had not been enough research yet to equip me with safer, more effective alternatives. I was even given an alter ego—as a future physician, I could not by definition be gay, and only marginally and hardly noticeably Latino—and therefore I was protected. I was supplied with excuses for my inability to act—I was no longer personally involved. In fact, it was imperative that I keep a professional distance from my patients so I could best serve them.

My own biases certainly colored my experience of medical school. I remained deeply conflicted about my choice of career, and longed to have more time to write poetry. It was easy to blame medical school itself for my unhappiness. In fact, I used the inflexibility and rigor of medical school to contain what I thought of as my wild, unacceptable impulses. Perhaps, I imagined, Harvard could make me straight, an upstanding citizen, more American, less likely to have AIDS. Perhaps by allowing myself to be distanced from people with AIDS, by doing research fifteen stories up in a monolithic concrete building dissecting rats' eyes under a microscope, I could improve my immunity, I could make myself blind to my connections to those dying people. If only I could take out my own eyes. If only I could trade in my poet's voicebox for that newfangled, anti-retroviral vocabulary, for a clean-cut physician's anatomically perfect larynx.

Moving to San Francisco from Boston, and from impressionable and repressed medical student status to self-styled new resident, had a great impact on my perceptions of my training. Ward 5A (referred to knowingly as "5-AIDS" by the housestaff in one of the hospitals where I nov work) is the place where people with AIDS are cared for by a dedicated group of nurses, doctors, social workers, and volunteers. It is for me the most oddly familiar place of all the oddly familiar places in the hospital. Late at night, after restarting an I.V. or evaluating a new fever, I have lingered in a patient's room to talk. Or in one particular case, to read Thom Gunn's poetry aloud—when we heard the respirator functioning in the plunging up-and-down iambics of "Lament," we nearly cried together. I have mixed my voice in among theirs. I have been fortunate to breathe in their sweet exhalations. I have, in fact, exchanged the same bodily secretions, albeit with others, but knowing somehow that all desire is the same. I may have even received the same person's blood by transfusion; ultimately, it is as though we were all from the same country.

In this spirit of connectedness, I thought once very briefly about teaching a poetry-writing workshop on the ward, during months when I would not be on-call—before I realized that these people, my patients, have been teaching *me* to write all along. Speaking all the more clearly and rarely through their oxygen masks, they demonstrate to me the parallel yet opposing processes of victimization and creativity: to tell me the story of their lives, it strikes me painfully as I jot down my medical histories, is for them to become authors of their very destinies. The circumstances under which they live, threatened by declining health caused by a virus for which we are told there is no cure, challenges them to remake their lives. Recounting the experience of sharing a needle, they have their hands on that needle again, they are existing before the virus entered their lives. They invent the cure with each narrative.

Indeed, they have taught me that when I write about AIDS, or about myself in relation to the virus, or about any patients' experiences, I am re-inventing the medical history I am obliged to take. Facts become mere possibilities; in another version, the patient lives to see her grandchildren, and the painful memory of her dead husband who contracted AIDS from a prostitute is retold, so that the unfaithful one is reconstituted, somehow, as human and forgivable. Possibilities, in turn, are created into facts; all along, right under our noses, AZT, or colostrum, or six hours of hopeful meditation a day have been the miracle cure just waiting to be discovered. AIDS, in the process of rendering people almost unable to talk, filling lungs with secretions and opportunistic infections, has at the same time brought the same people to an opportunity for an unmatchable eloquence, to retell their lives, to write the poems that will last forever in the troubled minds of future generations who will look back on the epidemic.

I have thought that, perhaps, by knowing and caring for these men and women I might assume just a bit of the greatness embodied by them, brought to the brink of death in their presence by the disease. At my most honest and terrified moments, what I really hope to gain is some control over the wildly destructive force the virus has become. The kind of control that comes with being at peace with the prospect of one's death. I wrote a sonnet not long ago which I devised to be a sort of contraption, a spring-locked box—a tiny coffin for the AIDS virus, I imagined—which I still re-read, even now, whenever I am overwhelmed by seeing the faces of my patients, and by unmistakable resemblance my own face, over and over again, among those of people dying of AIDS. It is an unrelenting, unforgiving love poem for a virus spread relentlessly by acts of desire for love. A condom made of words that can be used in retrospect, or better yet, an entirely new world wherein sex is gloriously only sex—condoms, viruses, and coffins unheard of—a world without the careful calculations of one's risk and the imagined, deadly repercussions.

So-called formal poetry holds the most appeal for me because in it are present the fundamental beating contents of the body at peace: the regularity of resting brainwave activity in contrast to the disorganized spiking of a seizure, the gentle ebb and flow of breathing, or sobbing, in contrast to the harsh spasmodic cough, the single-voiced, ringing chant of a slogan at a ACT UP rally in contrast to the indecipherable rumblings of AIDS funding debate on the Senate floor. The poem is a physical process, is bodily exercise: rhymes become the mental resting places in the ascending rhythmic stairway of memory. The poem perhaps is an idealization, or a dream of the physical—the imagined healthy form. Yet it does not renounce illness; rather, it reinterprets it as the beginning point for healing.

I wonder, then, whether poetry might also be therapeutic *per se.* Many of my friends, especially my collegues in medicine, have teased me for believing in the curative power of words, joking that I should write some doggerel on my prescriptions instead of the names of medications and directions for their use. If poetry is made of breath, or the beating heart, then surely it is not unreasonable to think it might reach those functions, however rarefied, in its audience. Moreover, I joke back, I have never seen a poem cause fulminant liver failure or bone marrow toxicity, even a really bad one. Putting the mouth to words, and by incantation reinstituting regular rhythms to the working lungs, these were the principles by which ancient healers in Native American cultures practiced their art. The Egyptians gave their dead a book full of charms and spells to be used in the afterlife—might not poetry, then, facilitate the passing to another realm? Poetry is a pulsing, organized imagining of what once was, or is to be. What life once was, what life is to be. It is ampules of the purest, clearest drug of all, the essence and distillation of the process of living itself.

I do not deny that most of the interventions Western medicine makes available to AIDS patients have their basis in scientific principles and truths, to the best that we can determine what those truths might be. In fact, I have even participated in delivering aggressive care to people with AIDS. I can only compare the feeling of placing an endotracheal tube in a patient in respiratory distress to the feeling of writing about the experience afterwards. A twenty-eight-year-old man most likely would have died before our eyes were it not for that tube. It was our explicit objective, after conferring as much as possible with him given the acuity of the situation, to save his life; he indicated that he wished to be intubated. As we sedated him (because he still contained so much life at that critical moment that he was able to fight the respirator) I watched his face change. He had lost his language: the endotracheal tube by anatomical necessity passes through the vocal cords in connecting the respirator to the airspaces of the lungs, thereby taking away one's ability to speak.

I am still not sure whether what he needed most during those last few days of his life was to speak or to breathe. The pneumonia which had made it so difficult for him to breathe on his own progressed rapidly, despite the various "big gun" antibiotics we infused into his veins. His fever climbed. We had given him a chance to live longer, reinstituting, if clumsily, the natural rhythm of breathing—had he survived the massive infection, the tube might have eventually come out—but it was at the cost of his last words. He died without last words. His parents flew in from New Jersey the night before he died, called in by his lover. They had not spoken in ten years, since the day he had told them he was gay and they threw him out in a rage. His mother stayed up all night, singing lullabies to him, comforting him, and perhaps herself, with small verses so familiarly rhymed. Hearing them comforted me too. When his blood pressure began to fall, quite suddenly, I imagined that his soul had already begun its departure, leaving his body only partly filled with the physical ingredients of life left behind, like powder in a loose sack. I imaged his soul, dancing away upon the rise and fall of his mother's quiet voice, each syllable a timid, graceful footfall.

Sometime later, perhaps weeks after he died, I heard his voice speak to me. It was in the form of a poem. The respirator and the lullaby were keeping time in the background, but what I heard most distinctly was his voice. He was breathing on his own again, and his breathing had taken on the quality of flight. Lying in my own bed, dreaming my dream of infinite blood, I imagined opening my eyes and seeing him standing naked before me. His entire body seemed to pulse with the poem he was creating. He was naming his body; his body was extremely beautiful, and I noticed every tiny imperfection, and cared deeply and attentively about it, as he spoke about the afterlife. It was as though he had left these words unspoken, and now they flowed over me so effortlessly I could almost understand them. I could almost understand a death caused by AIDS.

When I began writing about AIDS myself, I felt as though I was returning some of those words to the world. So much is unspoken—AIDS is not just a forbidden subject in most circles, it is absolutely unthinkable. Now, when I see SILENCE = DEATH painted on the sidewalk, or pinned to the lapel of my white coat, immediately I know what that means. It means our words *are* keeping us alive. Our words are the currency of our existence, the funds we spend to fight the disease, the blood that is spilled in the demonstrations, the tears shed and the semen ejaculated by and for our lovers. When I read Thom Gunn, or Marilyn Hacker, or J. D. McClatchy I am hearing this unthinkable but fiercely inhabited voice. A voice that does not wish simply to reclaim the body, but to celebrate it. A voice that desires fearlessly, without risks. A voice that heals. A voice from behind the respirator, from behind a mother's lips.

In ravaging our collective immunity, AIDS makes the naked body that much more clearly delineated, almost like beholding a person in the last stages of the disease. The spoken word becomes that much more urgent and honest, the poem that much more purely language. When addressing AIDS, the poet him/herself is no longer immune to the outer world, to its biases and hate. I have felt myself before the page to be utterly available, and this form of freedom is the hardest part, because it is the most terrifying freedom there is. The poetry of AIDS, then, is not simply and always about assuming control. Rewritten: it is about losing all control, it is about dying and fucking. Souls dissolving into songs, memories of a lost lover last seen in New Orleans, laments.

Sometimes I look to their bodies for a definitive answer to my ongoing prayer for understanding. I remember how I felt when I touched my grandfather's scars, those deep imprints left by Cuba: I was a blind child reading the past in Braille, understanding for the first time the vast plantation, the raging river, the cattle, the dark jail, and the soldiers' clubs. When I ask my patients to undress, I think of him. I touch the skin, feel the texture, the warmth of a new purple spot. I examine the breast, collect a bit of the discharge. The heart sounds always seem louder, more urgent, but I wonder whether that is because so many have already lost so much weight, their hearts only barely beneath the surface. I listen to the abdomen digesting everything, the internal, constant interface with the outside world. I try desperately not to desire them, because it is unprofessional, and because it is too human and scary and powerful. I imagine having their bodies, though, possessing them as I do my own, occupying that same space. It feels exactly the same, except perhaps it is more wonderful to be naked (even in the air-conditioned, too-metallic office the hospital provides me). Maybe I am only feeling free of my usual armor, my needle-hands and ophthalmoscope-eyes transformed to soft fingers and gentle, green irises. Funny how I never feel the pain, though I can often reproduce it in them as I press and poke the indicated region. Pain must be too personal, held too deeply with the body, to be known without actually experiencing it. Though my grandfather's smile emphasized a certain scar on his forehead, and therefore could feel like a blow to the head, so bitter and full of loss, I never felt the pain he must have known. I can only imagine it.

Seeing their bodies makes me remember a priest's sermon I heard when I was a small child in Venezuela. A blinding white church, all right angles, dusty, vibrant heat, red-tiled floor, roughly hewn wooden pews that might give you a splinter. It was a eulogy of sorts. He was asking us to imagine Christ's suffering on the cross. How willing we all were, closing our eyes tightly, driving the nails through our hands and feet, allowing the spear into our livers, the air-conditioner humming as we sat enraptured, silent. Was I willing to die for my sins? For the sins of others? I wondered at the common experience of imagining such pain and suffering. I wondered whether people were really feeling Christ's wounds, or whether like me they were recalling to their minds the times when they had cut themselves with a sharp knife they should not have been using in the first place, or fell off a bicycle—or, since they were mostly women, whether they were remembering their breast cancer surgery or their husbands beating them. Some *viejitas* up in front began moaning gently, then sobbing. The spell was broken suddenly when the priest loudly scolded us: *No!* he shouted, Christ's suffering was a mystery and utterly unknowable. Only through faith could we achieve redemption, and it was the relief of pain through God's forgiveness that was to be our eternal reward in heaven. As he became more and more animated, his voice rising toward indignation and anger and salvation, I lost myself staring at the emaciated peeling figure above the alter, crucified for the benefit of our eyes and souls. I have lost myself the same way in the faces, the bodies, and the poems of people with AIDS. I see them teaching us, each one of us, the meaning of our own losses. Teaching us that every word is true.

A SHALLOW POOL
OF TIME

Fran Peavey

Fran Peavey is a writer and social activist whose involvement in global issues pre-dates her HIV diagnosis. A co-founder of Interhelp, an international network of activists interested in the spiritual, psychological, and political dimensions of social change, she travels around the world learning from and advising other activists. Peavey is the author of three books, *Heart Politics, By Life's Grace,* and *A Shallow Pool of Time,* which records her insights into the personal, political, and spiritual dimensions of AIDS. She lives in Oakland, California.

I love to walk among great, old trees. Last summer a friend took me to a maple forest in Vermont. As we walked my friend told me that a healthy maple tree has a full leaf pattern in its outer perimeter, so its outline creates a solid, rather smooth line. You don't see spaces between the branches. From the jagged line of foliage on nearly all of the trees, it was easy to see that this forest was gravely ill. Like other forests in Canada and the Northeastern United States it has been poisoned by acid rain.

I hear that three-quarters of the people in my spiritual community in San Francisco have the AIDS virus in their blood. On Sundays when I stand to sing, I look around and sense that

I am standing in a dying forest. I miss trees from month to month. Friends are falling all around me.

We live in a world that is too polluted., There is not enough of an ozone layer left to protect us. Too much radioactivity has been released. New viruses mutate or are man-made; new conditions threaten our species.

It seems that we do not yet know how to mourn and let go when a whole way of life begins to die. Even when we can see that death, can know it from inside, it is difficult to believe that a new way of life must and will emerge. In these last years of the twentieth century, our old way of life has already begun its terminal decline, and yet we do not see a new birth arising.

We do not know how to mourn this death. So automatically, and in something of a frenzy, we cling to that which is mostly dead. It is our clinging that most surely will kill us, or at least speed the downward spiral.

Maybe we people who carry the AIDS virus are the canaries in the mine. Maybe we can whistle such a true and sweet song that our species will see that we must get out of the mine; we must change our addiction to consumption, pollution and mindlessness.

I, and thousands like me with viruses in our bodies, are waiting. This is not a passive waiting: we are not resigned to death. In many ways, we are busy doing whatever we can to increase our chances of "beating this thing," as Dennis put it. But there is a lot of waiting, too.

When I visited South Africa in 1986, I saw an entire society that was, in a sense, waiting. The black South Africans I spoke with showed a curious mixture of hope and hopelessness. They wait for possibility of change in the social contract between peoples. The white South Africans wait for that, too–sensing, perhaps dreading, the deep suffering and change that is in store for them when the inevitable spark comes. But they find hope within hopelessness as they look north at Zimbabwe where whites and blacks have passed through a revolution and now live in a new social arrangement where both racial groups participate in decisions in a way that is new for them.

The South Africans' way of waiting—of carrying on with faith and hope in the face of individually hopeless situations—was a perspective I personally had only dimly understood. It became clearer to me this summer as I wrestled with the waiting that lay before me, as I wondered what this AIDS virus was doing in my body. Contemplating my own future and our collective future—both very much in doubt—I asked myself, "How can I learn to wait, to sit with the devastating information which I now know?"

When I give talks or do comedy shows, people often approach me afterward to ask me about the future. They take me to a corner of the room and quietly say, "I hear that the environment is so destroyed that it cannot be reversed, that the end has already begun. Is that true?" They think somehow a comedian will know! Turning to comedians with questions like that is like putting clowns at the health centres to tell people whether they are HIV-positive. (Maybe that's not a bad idea!) What can I tell these people? I have read about studies by the Worldwatch Institute and by the United Nations which indicate that some parts of our ecosystems and some species have been irreversibly destroyed. But who can know the extent of the damage? Our physical world is so complex and interconnected that the ramifications of any deterioration are significant and, I suspect, more extensive than most of us can comprehend.

And so we wait. Our waiting is directed toward a questionable future, one that seems to be closing in on the present and making it untenable. We are waiting for something we really don't want. We do everything we can to postpone the expected future. A friend of mine told me that before he knew he was HIV positive he jogged furiously every day, hoping that he could "outrun" the virus. As a species, we try to clean up toxic waste dumps and stop the clear cutting of the forests. We make every effort to preserve our health and our planet, but we also must wait, knowing the virus is already in the system, not yet knowing whether it is terminal or not. All actions may increase the odds that the ecosystem will not collapse completely before key changes can be brought into place.

Still, this waiting can feel like a passive activity. It produces in us feelings of powerlessness and vulnerability–infantile feelings–and we hate that. We rage against our powerlessness, our vulnerability, our having to wait. It is this rage that fuels the discussion of violent strategies in the AIDS community. In both instances, the rage is born of despair and a weariness of waiting while suffering continues.

In our times, there is a prevalent sense of "resignation," as Robert Lifton calls it. I occasionally taste the pungent flavour of that resignation myself. I have been looking at this resignation, within me, exploring it, trying to find out how to work with that resignation in order to allow my beak to harden so I can peck my way out of my egg and grow up and fly. It is a very tough task. In the early days of working against nuclear war and environmental destruction, I decided to ask myself every day the strategic question, "What can I do to help the world survive?" Since then I have made it my practice to get up usually between four and five in the morning sitting for an hour with that question, as well as practising loving people I am separated from.

I thought in 1979 that I might have to ask this question for many years without receiving any ideas from that life force inside and outside me. But I was willing to give the life force an opportunity to create answers and to develop my will by first walking answerless into the void of my morning sitting., I was prepared to do that for ten years without an answer. I said to myself that if at the end of that time no answer had come, I would re-evaluate. This is the tenth year of that practice.

Fortunately some answers have arrived including comedy and other projects that I work on today. To be willing to ask strategic questions to which there are no known answers, and to wait—those are among the most difficult and heroic tasks we can do now. To continue to ask and consult that universal life force to direct us is, I believe, one of the most valuable beak-hardening and spiritually maturing tasks we can do in our time.

We also must be willing to do whatever the life-force-from-within suggests. Often only a small thing comes clear in the morning meditation. I think it's important to carry out those small ideas in order to develop my "doing" muscles—to prove to myself and to the earth that I am standing ready. I am ready to make peace with my family members and friends; to do those intimate peacemaking tasks that are an ongoing part of life. At the same time, when big jobs come, I work through my shyness and small concept of myself enough to be able to say, "I'm ready."

When the opportunity came to help clean the Ganges, it was a real stretch for me and my small-town-Idaho sense of myself, but I had to say, "I'm ready." I wait, standing ready, asking every day for direction for the life force planted inside of me—and inside all beings—that can make a great difference in this crucial time.

Each of us can only do a very little to help the whole situation, but each small piece plays an important part in creating the whole shift.

It is important how we carry this waiting. Start paying attention to how you wait, the cost on your soul and the cost of this waiting on life around you. Find a way to smile on that waiting. For me, this is where my comedy comes from. I very much appreciate Thich Nhat Hanh's suggestion that we learn to smile on our own and others' suffering—not smiling derisively, but smiling as a way of joining ourselves to the suffering.

T. S. Eliot writes in his poem "East Coker" about waiting:

I said to my soul, be still, and wait without
   hope
For hope would be hope for the wrong thing;
   wait without love
For love would be love of the wrong thing;
   there is yet faith
But the faith and the love and the hope are all
   in the waiting.
Wait without thought, for you are not ready for
   thought:
So the darkness shall be the light, and the stillness the
   dancing.

It is so important to keep laughing in the midst of our waiting, in the midst of our fears and morbidity. Whatever we are dying of individually and collectively, whatever is happening to our forests, it is a key spiritual posture to smile upon our human condition. This, of course, does not preclude crying for the grief in the death, trembling with fear or raging in anger.

How can we allow the life force to inform and inspire us? We learn to wait and take very careful care of that bomb we carry inside of us. We can look at each other in our meetings and on the street. We can recognize each other. We are surrounded by people who are working to develop the muscle to do what has to be done—moving individually and collectively to meet the need. The old is dead, the new is not yet ready to be born. We are in the in-between time and so we wait.

We ask ourselves what time it is in our individual lives and in the life of our species. And we realize that we don't know. We tell ourselves stories, we lose ourselves in the whirl of everyday activities, we pretend that we are indifferent about the waiting and the toll it takes on us, we rehearse death's arrival, we affirm our faith in a transcendent power, we pray to spirits to intercede for us in the molding of the future. We invent magic and rituals to help us explore the meaning of waiting. But still we must wait.

Waiting becomes an allegory, a private purgatory in which our moral and psychic fibre is tested. We learn from waiting. We become disciplined, tough, hardened, stoic. And yet, in this waiting together we also find a kind of intimacy and loving that is rare in ordinary life. We experience interconnectedness. We are surprised by feelings of intense joy as we stand in a momentary shard of light.

Someday, perhaps, we will all be able to see what a non-political event this epidemic is; that it is not a matter of which populations are suffering and how far they are from our own; that no one is really unaffected. What a sweet illumination that will be! Come with me to a time distant in the future when our species can look back and see these present times, the AIDS virus, the people infected and afraid, the people non-infected and afraid, where we can see it all as past. How will our times look from a perspective in which we, fragile and vulnerable as well as strong and tough beings now walking the streets in our tennis shoes, will be but dust for historians? Our plague will surely look much like plagues of other times—the black plague, the bubonic plague, polio and others. For AIDS too will be conquered, and new problems will arise until the earth is restored to health and the people learn to live together within reasonable limits of resources.

Someday we may know with confidence that our species is making the changes necessary for humans to live, and we may return in time to the normal mysteries of existence, love and a personal death in the natural order of things.

SEX, DRUGS, ROCK-N-ROLL, AND AIDS

Iris de la Cruz

Iris de la Cruz died of AIDS on May 11, 1991, at the age of 37. She was an active member of P.O.N.Y. (Prostitutes of New York) and worked as an emergency medical technician and facilitator of support groups for bisexuals and heterosexuals diagnosed with HIV.

I remember seeing the prostitutes on Third Avenue. I started getting high with them and before long I was out there turning tricks. I thought it was great. I had enough money to take care of both my heroin habit and my child and to maintain an apartment on East Fourteenth Street. I walked to work at night! By this time I was taking courses at the School of Visual Arts and shooting up before school in the bathroom. My daughter was attending day care (which was affiliated with the Puerto Rican Socialist Party—old habits die hard). And I thought I was doing all right.

When I started hustling, most of the women were white. Nobody turned a trick for less than $25, and if you were picked up for loitering, they let you out in the morning. They even had a squad of cops, known as the "pussy posse," to round up the whores. I thought I had it made. I liked the feeling of power having men honk their horns as I walked the streets. And the idea that these men thought I was pretty enough to pay me for sex was a big ego boost. This went on for years with the drug habit increasing subtly.

During this time I started writing and got a job writing columns on drugs and sex for men's magazines. This was the mid–1970s, and drugs and disco were considered very chic. All the good parties had lines of coke on coffee tables, and sex clubs were making millions. The party continued. Same faces, different drugs. My drug usage escalated. I dropped out of college and sent my daughter to San Francisco to live with her father. I still kept writing.

My editor set up a meeting with a woman who was organizing prostitutes out on the West Coast, and she asked me if I was interested in reviving P.O.N.Y. (Prostitutes of New York). My best friend had just been found nude, under the Brooklyn Bridge, with her throat cut. We used to watch each other's backs out on the stroll. Hookers needed to be protected, since it was obvious the police and government thought we were expendable. I became the spokesperson for P.O.N.Y. and did all kinds of interviews. The media has always been enthralled with articulate "street people." I kept the ratings up. This went on for about a year while I spent more and more time in shooting galleries. Finally, the unions started getting interested in prostitutes, and P.O.N.Y. started becoming enmeshed in politics. I walked away.

A couple of years passed, and my drug habit became the only thing I was interested in. I lost my apartment and was basically living in shooting galleries. I was still hustling, but the wait between tricks became longer and longer. I looked and acted like your basic run-of-the-mill junkie. I had amassed twenty-six arrests, two of them for second-degree assault. I had meant it when I said that no one was ever gonna beat me. I became real good with a knife and felt nothing cutting someone. I felt nothing anyway. If I called my daughter and any feelings of love or regret came up, I would sedate myself. My life consisted of getting high (I was now addicted to heroin, methadone, sleeping pills, and tranquilizers) and turning tricks. Emotions were not something I wanted to deal with. I used to pray to die. I'd overdose almost every month and then raise hell with hospital staff for reviving me. I tried getting into drug treatments, but they were overcrowded and had waiting lists.

This was a very exciting time in my life. Too bad I wasn't there to experience it. I had a boyfriend I really did love (I just wasn't wild about myself). So there was someone to watch my back and get high with. But I was getting tired. There is nothing more pitiful than an old junkie whore.

It was about this time that I started noticing that a lot of my friends were getting sick and dying. When I had to be hospitalized for pelvic inflammatory disease, the rage kicked up again. I returned to the streets with a vengeance and became known as La Blanca Loca (the crazy white woman). I fought with everyone until in a spaced-out rage I stabbed a man that tried to rip me off.

I was given one and one-half to three years. I kicked all the drugs in jail, complete with convulsions, vomiting, and diarrhea. I hated being locked up, and it occurred to me that the main reason people are locked away is because they're a threat either to themselves or to society. On drugs, I was both. I copped to a program after spending eight months dealing with the insanity the New York State Department of Corrections is notorious for. It was time to start over.

I stayed in treatment for about nine months and learned some very important things, like how to channel my rage, and loving support, and encounter groups. I learned how to accept and give love. I also learned why so many of my friends were dying. We started losing people in the program. The enemy finally had a name. It was AIDS.

After I left treatment I took a course and got my license as an emergency medical technician. I had been drug free for some time and was making Narcotics Anonymous meetings. So I worked as an EMT with plans to someday go through medical school. After years of destructive behavior, I really felt I had to pay back for the very fact that I was still alive. I guess it's true what they say about the Lord protecting fools and children. So I worked, and tried to ignore the little things that kept cropping up, such as the white stuff in my mouth and the fatigue.

I used to transport AIDS patients a lot, since I was the only one that didn't give the dispatcher a hard time about it. By this time they were finding out that the disease wasn't airborne, and it was only transmitted by bodily fluids. So I would wear gloves but refused to wear a mask or "suit up" to transport AIDS patients. Emergency Room nurses would run all kinds of guilt trips about what I was bringing home to my family. I once had a big fight with a charge nurse after I suctioned a patient in the E.R. with PCP. He was left for over an hour all congested. Medical staff, on the whole, resented AIDS patients. The feeling was that they were all faggots and dope fiends and deserved what they got. By this time, I knew what the signs and symptoms were. I knew I was positive for the AIDS virus.

I was still working, even though I was tired all the time. Finally I had a patient go into cardiac arrest in the back of an ambulance. The man had a urinary obstruction and was semi-comatose. I panicked and started CPR without a mask. I found out later he had active tuberculosis. A few weeks later, after working with soaring fevers, I had to be hospitalized.

My temperature was spiking up to 105.5 degrees, and the nurses were telling my mother to stay with me because I would not make it through the night. I was delirious and spoke with my father and grandmother. They're both dead. But I made it; I guess I'm too much of a bitch to die.

I got out of the hospital ninety days later looking like the national AIDS poster child. I spent the next ten months getting my weight and strength back. Locked in my mom's house, I felt like a germ. Back to feeling ugly and unloved. I didn't want to be touched because I felt unclean. In this society women's bodies are unclean and have to be deodorized before they're acceptable. So now, on top of everything, I was diseased. My mother wouldn't hear it. She kept hugging me despite the fact that I shied away, began attending a mothers' group, and forced me to go out. My first time on a train I sat there looking at lovers and families and thinking that these options are closed to me. I would look at the person next to me and think, "Would they still sit next to me if they knew I had AIDS?"

I started attending a group for women with HIV. I felt like I was the only woman in the world with AIDS. It was all gay white men. This group changed that.

All of a sudden I discovered other women with the virus. There were black women, white women, Latinas, rich women, and poor women. There were addicts and transfusion women. They were mothers and sisters and lovers and daughters and grandmothers. Some were militant lesbians and others were Republicans (imagine that! Even Republicans get AIDS). And we were all connected by the virus. Outside differences became trivial; feelings and survival were everyone's main concern. And I learned that there was still a lot of love left in me. The rage mellowed.

I was diagnosed with AIDS two years ago. I kept attending the women's group until the leader left. Then I took over the facilitator's role along with my best friend, Helen, who has ARC. A few months ago I started a group for bi- and heterosexuals dealing with HIV. I do AIDS outreach and education. I teach safer sex and show addicts how to clean their works. I encourage them to seek treatment. The rage that burned is now a hot anger. I've been to too many funerals with this disease. I'm tired of the newly diagnosed being made to feel dirty. I'm tired of my people being neglected and left dying on the streets. My child is now nineteen and we're very close. The legacy I want to leave her is for her to remember her mama was a survivor. She survived drugs and she survived her own worst enemy, which was herself. And she taught others survival. She may or may not have survived AIDS, but she kicked ass while she was here.

TO MY READERS

Harold Brodkey

Harold Brodkey's recent nonfiction has concerned his own AIDS diagnosis, and much of it has appeared in *The New Yorker*. He is also the author of the novels *The Runaway Soul* and *Profane Friendship,* and two collections of short fiction, *First Love and Other Sorrows* and *Stories in an Almost Classical Mode.* He lives in New York City with his wife, the writer Ellen Schwamm.

I have AIDS. I am surprised that I do. I have not been exposed since the nineteen-seventies, which is to say that my experiences, my adventures in homosexuality took place largely in the nineteen-sixties, and back then I relied on time and abstinence to indicate my degree of freedom from infection and to protect others and myself.

At first, shadows and doubts of various kinds disturbed my sleep, but later I felt more certainty of safety. Before AIDS was identified, I thought five years without noticeable infection would indicate one was without disease. When AIDS was first identified, five years was held to indicate safety. That changed. Twenty years now is considered a distance in time that might indicate safety, but a slight number of AIDS cases are anomalous; that is, the delay in illness is not explicable within the assumed rules, even under the most careful, cynical investigation. It doesn't matter much. I have AIDS. I have had *Pneumocystis carinii* pneumonia, which almost killed me. Unlikely or not, blood test, T-cell count, the fact that it was *Pneumocystis* means I have AIDS and must die.

There it is. At the time I was told, I was so ill, so racked with fever and having such difficulty breathing, that I hardly cared. I was embarrassed and shamed that the people who cared for me in the hospital had to take special precautions to protect themselves. Then as the fever went down I suppose my pride and sense of competition took over. When someone from social services showed up to offer counsel, I found that bothersome, although the counsellor was a very fine person, warm and intelligent. I suppose I was competitive with or antagonistic toward the assumption that now my death would be harder than other deaths, harder to bear, and that the sentence to such death and suffering was unbearable.

I didn't find it so. I didn't want to find it so. Granted, I am perverse. But my head felt the doom was bearable. My body hurt. I haven't felt even halfway human for eight or nine weeks now, until the last two or three days. It was as if I had walked through a door into the most unstable physical state of wretched and greatly undesirable discomfort possible.

But, of course, blindness and dementia are worse states. And my parents suffered excruciatingly with heart trouble and cancer. Also, I was not, am not, young. I am not being cut down before I have had a chance to live. Most important, I was not and am not alone. On the second day, when the truth was known, my wife, Ellen Schwamm, moved into the hospital with me. When we began to tell the family, no one rejected me. No one. I am embarrassed to be ill and to be ill in this way, but no one yet has shown disgust or revulsion. I expect it. But in the hospital AIDS is a boring thing for internes, it is so common. And outside it arouses, at least in New York, sympathy and curiosity. I do get the feeling I am a bit on show, or rather my death is and my moods are. But so what?

So far the worst moments, in terms of grief, came about when I was visited by my grandson, aged four, a wide-faced blond, a second child, bright, and rather expert at emotional warfare. I hadn't seen him in four months, and he looked at me snottily and said, "I don't remember *you.*" I said, "I used to be a pink-and-black horse." He looked at me, thought or reacted, then grinned and said, "I remember you now," and came over and took my hand and generally didn't leave my side. But the horror was I had no strength to respond or pretend after only a short while, less than an hour. I am not able to be present for him and never will be anymore. That led to a bad twenty-four hours. But that can hardly be uncommon, and I had already felt a version of it toward Ellen, although less intense, because I am able to be there in some ways still, and can find some sort of robot strength in myself still if I have to.

My doctor, who is very able and very experienced, is surprised that I am not more depressed. He says cheerfully that I am much more upset than I realize. He credits some of the medicines with shielding me, my mood, and warns me that severe unhappiness is coming, but so far it hasn't come. I have resisted it, I suppose. And my wife is with me every moment. I feel cut off from old age, it's true, but that's not like someone young feeling cut off from most of his or her possible life.

In my adult life and in my childhood, I was rarely, almost never ill, but when I was, it was always serious, and nearly fatal. I have been given up by my doctors three times in my life and for a few mintues a fourth time. This time is more convincing but otherwise it is not an unfamiliar or unexplained territory.

I was a hypochondriac, but for a good reason—I could take no medicine, none at all, without extreme, perverse, or allergic reactions. Essentially I never got sick. I was gym-going, hike-taking, cautious, oversensitive to the quality of the air, to heat and cold, noise and odors, someone who felt tireder more quickly than most people because of all these knife-edge reactions, someone who was careful not to get sick, because my allergic reactions to medicines made almost any illness a drastic experience.

I had an extremely stable baseline of mood and of mind, of mental *landscape*. Well, that's gone; it's entirely gone. From the moment my oxygen intake fell to about fifty per cent and the ambulance drivers arrived in our apartment with a gurney and with oxygen for me to breathe, from that moment and then in the hospital until now, I have not had even one moment of physical stability. I am filled off-and-on with surf noises as if I were a seashell, my blood seems to fizz and tingle. I have low and high fevers. For a day I had a kind of fever with chills and sweats but with body temperature *below* normal, at 96 degrees. I have choked and had trouble breathing. I have had pleuritis, or pleurisy, in my right lung, an inflammation of the thoracic cavity which feels like a burning stiffness of the muscles and which hurt like hell if I coughed, moved suddenly, or reached to pick something up.

And, or course, one can die at any moment or discover symptoms of some entirely new disease. My life has changed into this death, irreversibly.

But I don't *think* the death sentence bothers me. I don't see why it should more than before. I have had little trouble living with the death-warrant aspect of life until now. I never denied, never hysterically defined the reality of death, the presence and idea of it, the inevitability of it. I always knew *I* would die. I never felt invulnerable or immortal. I felt the presence and menace of death in bright sunlight and in the woods and in moments of danger in cars and planes. I felt it in others' lives. Fear and rage toward death for me is focussed on resisting death's soft jaws at key moments, fighting back the interruption, the separation. In physical moments when I was younger, I had great surges of wild strength when in danger, mountain

climbing, for instance, or threatened in a fight or by muggers in
the city. In the old days I would put my childish or young
strength at the service of people who were ill. I would lend
them my will power, too. Death scared me some, maybe even
terrified me in a way, but at the same time I had no great fear
of death. Why should it be different now? Ought I to crack up
because a bluff has been called?

As with other children, when I was very young, death was
interesting—dead insects, dead birds, dead people. In a middle-
class, upper-middle-class milieu, everything connected to real
death was odd, I mean in relation to pretensions and state-
ments, projects and language and pride. It seemed softly
adamant, an undoing, a rearrangement, a softly meddlesome
and irresistible silence. It was something some boys I knew and
I thought we ought to familiarize ourselves with. Early on, and
also in adolescence, we had a particular, conscious will not to
be controlled by fear of death—there were things we would die
rather than do. To some extent this rebelliousness was also controlled; to some extent we could choose our dangers, but not
always. All this may be common among the young during a
war; I grew up during the Second World War. And a lot was
dependent on locality, and social class, the defense of the sexual self or the private self against one's father or in school.

Having accepted death long ago in order to be physically
and morally free—to some extent—I am not crushed by this final
sentence of death, at least not yet, and I don't think it is denial.
I think my disbelief weeks ago gave way to the *maybe so* of the
onset of belief. I am sick and exhausted, numbed and darkened,
by my approximate dying a few weeks ago from *Pneumocystis,*
and consider death a silence, a silence and a privacy and an
untouchability, as no more reactions and opinions, as a relief, a
privilege, a lucky and graceful and symmetrical silence to be
grateful for. The actual words I used inwardly read ambiguous-
ly when written out—*it's about time* for silence.

I'm sixty-two, and it's ecological sense to die while you're still productive, die and clear a space for others, old and young. I didn't always appreciate what I had at the time, but I am aware now that accusations against me or being lucky in love were pretty much true and of being lucky sexually, also true. And lucky intellectually and, occasionally, lucky in the people I worked with. I have no sad stories about love or sex.

And I think my work will live. And I am tired of defending it, tired of giving my life to it. But I have liked my life. I like my life at present, being ill. I like the people I deal with. I don't feel I am being whisked off the stage or murdered and stuffed in a laundry hamper while my life is incomplete. It's my turn to die—I can see that that is interesting to some people but not that it is tragic. Yes, I was left out of some things and was cheated over a lifetime in a bad way but who isn't and so what? I had a lot of privileges as well. Sometimes I'm sad about its being over but I'm that way about books and sunsets and conversations. The medicines I take don't grant my moods much independence, so I suspect these reactions, but I think they are my own. I have been a fool all my life, giving away large chunks of time and wasting years on nothing much, and maybe I'm being a fool now.

And I have died before, come close enough to dying that doctors and nurses on those occasions said those were death experiences, the approach to death, a little of death felt from the inside. And I have nursed dying people and been at deathbeds. I nearly died when my first mother did; I was two years old. As an adult, at one point, I forced myself to remember what I could of the child's feelings. The feelings I have now are far milder. My work, my notions and theories and doctrines, my pride have conspired to make me feel as I do now that I am ill.

I have always remembered nearly dying when I was seven and had an allergic, hypothermic reaction coming out of anesthesia. When I was thirty, a hepatitis thing was misdiagnosed as cancer of the liver, and I was told I had six weeks to live. The sensations at those various times were not much alike, but the feeling of extreme sickness, of being racked, was and is the same as is the sense of the real death.

I have wondered at times if maybe my resistance to the fear-of-death wasn't laziness and low mental alertness, a cowardly inability to admit that horror was horror, that dying was unbearable. It feels, though, like a life-giving rebelliousness, a kind of blossoming. Not a love of death but maybe a love of God. I wouldn't want to be hanged and it would kill my soul to be a hangman but I always hoped that if I were hanged I would be amused and superior, and capable of having a good time somehow as I died—this may be a sense of human style in an orphan, greatly damaged and deadened, a mere sense of style overriding a more normal terror and sense of an injustice of destiny. Certainly, it is a *dangerous* trait. I am not sensible...At all times I am more afraid of anesthesia and surgery than I am of death. I have had moments of terror, of abject fear. I was rather glad to have those moments. But the strain was tremendous. My feelings of terror have had a scattered quality mostly, and I tended to despise them as petty. I have more fear of cowardice and of being broken by torture than I do of death. I am aware of my vulnerability, of how close I come to being shattered. But next to that is a considerable amount of nerve—my blood parents and real grandparents were said to have been insanely brave, to have had an arrogant sang-froid about their courage and what it allowed them to do. They had, each of them, a strong tropism toward the epic. My mother, before I was born, travelled alone from near Leningrad to Illinois in the nineteen-twenties, a journey that, at her social level, took nearly two months; the year before, her older brother had disappeared, perhaps murdered. My father once boxed a dozen men in a row one evening on a bet and supposedly laid all the women under thirty who lined up afterward. Another time, bet-

ter attested, with two other men, he took on a squad of march-
ing local Nazis in St. Louis, twenty-five or thirty men, and won.

I myself am a coward, oversensitive, lazy, reclusive, but the
mind and spirit have their requirement of independence; and
death can't help but seem more bearable than a stupid life of
guilt, say.

Is death other than silence and nothingness? In my experiences of it, it is that disk of acceptance and of unthreading and
disappearance at the bottom of the chute of revenant memories, ghosts and the living, the gantlet of important recollec-
tions through which one is forced in order to approach the end
of one's consciousness. Death itself is soft, softly lit, vastly dark.
The self becomes taut with metamorphosis and seems to give
off some light and to have a not-quite-great-enough fearlessness
toward that immensity of the end of individuality, toward one's
absorption into the dance of particles and inaudibility. Living,
one undergoes one metamorphosis after another—often, they
are cockroach states inset with moments of passivity, with the
sense of real death—but they are continuous and linked. This
one is a stillness and represents a sifting out of identity and its
stories, a breaking off or removal of the self, and a devolution
into mere effect and memory, outspread and not tightly bound
but scattered among micromotions and as if more windblown
than in life.

People speak of wanting to live to see their grandchildren
marry, but what is it they will see? A sentimental ceremony or
a real occasion involving real lives? Life is a kind of horror. It
is O.K., but it is wearing. Enemies and thieves don't lay off as
you weaken. The wicked flourish by being ruthless even then.
If you are ill, you have to have a good lawyer. Depending on
your circumstances, in some cases you have to back off and lie
low. You're weak. Death is preferable to daily retreat.

Certainly people on the street who smile gently at me as I
walk slowly or X-ray attendants calling me *darling* or *lovey* are

aware of this last thing. A woman I know who died a few years back spoke of this in relation to herself. She hated it. I don't want to talk about my dying to everyone, or over and over. Is my attitude only vanity—and more vanity—in the end? In a sense, I steal each day, but I steal it by making no effort. It is just there, sunlight or rain, nightfall or morning. I am still living at least a kind of life, and I don't want to be reduced to an image now, or, in my own mind, feel I am spending all my time on my dying instead of on living, to some satisfying extent, the time I have left.

Not constantly but not inconstantly either, underneath the sentimentality and obstinacy of my attitudes, are, as you might expect, a quite severe rage and a vast, a truly extensive terror, anchored in contempt for you and for life and for everything. But let's keep that beast in its gulf of darkness. Let's be polite and proper and devoted to life now as we were earlier in our life on this planet.

One of the things that struck me when I was first told that I had AIDS was that I was cut off from my family inheritance of fatal diseases—the strokes and high blood pressure and cancers and tumors of my ancestors. My medical fate is quite different; I felt a bit orphaned yet again, and idiosyncratic, but strangely also as if I had been invited, almost abducted, to a party, a sombre feast but not entirely grim, a feast of the seriously afflicted who yet were at war with social indifference and prejudice and hatred. It seemed to me that I was surrounded by braveries without number, that I had been inducted into a phalanx of the wildly-alive-even-if-dying, and I felt honored that I would, so to speak, die in the company of such people.

Really, I can say nothing further at this point. Pray for me.

FEAR OF
AIDS
KILLED SARAH

Christine Boose

Christine Boose, 18, attended City-as-School High School and, in 1992, testified at a public hearing on Chancellor Joseph Fernandez's proposal to distribute condoms in New York City schools and to improve and update the AIDS education program for city high school students.

I lost my best friend Sarah to this crazy, mysterious disease called AIDS. Yes, the same one we all think we're immune to because it only affects people who sleep around, or better yet, people who are gay.

Well, Sarah was 19. She graduated from high school and wanted to go to college to become a fashion designer. Her boyfriend Charlie was 22. They were going out for a year and four months.

Sarah was the nicest person to talk to. She always knew what to say when I was upset. She was always giving me advice, which is typical of a best friend.

Sarah didn't sleep around. She had only four boyfriends all her life, and generally, she was careful about sex. I mean, she normally used condoms, except, I guess, sometimes she "slipped."

Sarah called me at the end of September and told me she not only thought she was pregnant, but hoped that she was. She got a pregnancy test and was very happy to find out that in fact, she was pregnant.

That was such a beautiful day. Charlie proposed marriage and everything. Sarah and Charlie planned to get married the day before Christmas. We were all so happy.

The next day, Sarah went to see her family doctor for a check-up. He advised her to get a complete physical, including a test for HIV (the virus that causes AIDS). When the results came back, Sarah found out she was HIV-positive. She knew that her baby was at risk of becoming HIV-infected, so she decided to have an abortion. Now, when I think about it, I can't believe how fast everything happened.

Charlie also got tested and found out he was HIV-positive too.

Sarah and Charlie didn't bother blaming each other. They just went straight into a deep depression. Sarah and I saw a lot of each other then, and spoke on the phone all the time. I was the only friend that really stuck around when everybody else sort of disappeared.

Sarah was very confused. She knew too little about HIV, and she had too many questions, too many doubts, too many ugly thoughts. Since I was one of the only people she would talk to, I became very frustrated because I didn't know much about HIV myself. In other words, I didn't have all the answers and I felt very responsible.

So I decided to go for counseling in my school, City-as-School, and it helped me feel better. My AIDS coordinator told me that it was important for Sarah to seek counseling as well, because it would help her deal with the problems she was facing as they came along.

I spoke to Sarah about how important it was that she get counseling, but she wouldn't listen. She said she didn't want to speak to anyone besides me—she didn't want to tell anyone. I also spoke with Sarah's mother and she agreed with me that counseling was important in Sarah's case, simply because we didn't know how to help her. However, all our efforts were useless.

Sarah still didn't want to speak to anyone except her mom, her boyfriend, and me. She was afraid everyone else would feel disgusted by her and reject her. She was so afraid of the stigma of AIDS and the disease itself. She felt that the time between becoming HIV-infected and actually having any symptoms or even AIDS was like a rotting period. To Sarah it was all the same as death, whether it was slow or quick, painless or not. She felt she was going to die and that's all that mattered. She was obsessed.

Sarah talked a lot about killing herself. She said she lost the will to do anything since she found out she didn't have a long way to go. I didn't think she'd really do it, but I thought if I was in her position, I'd probably think about suicide too.

On the 8th of October, Sarah called and and we talked for four hours. She said she was going to do it—she wanted to kill herself that night. I didn't know what to tell her. I didn't want her to die and I told her that. But her response was, "What's the difference if I wait until I rot or just do it now!"

Poor Sarah. I wish I could have told her that so many people live for years being HIV-positive before actually getting AIDS and that there are ways of taking care of yourself, of being happy.

Sarah died that night. She turned on the oven, took some sleeping pills, and went to sleep for good. Nobody else was in the house.

Charlie now lives with Sarah's mother in Texas. Although he's HIV-positive, he's very hopeful. He lives a normal life and while he's still very upset, he'll be all right.

I never thought much about AIDS until Sarah became

HIV-infected. It seemed so remote. However, AIDS is a reality. It's actually very close to us. Until Sarah, I didn't even know the difference between HIV and AIDS. Now I know that you could be infected with HIV for up to 10 years, sometimes without any symptoms, before you develop full-blown AIDS. This means that if someone gets AIDS when she's in her 20s, chances are she contracted the virus in her teens.

That makes AIDS dangerous to us teenagers. I guess what I mean is that we're all at risk—everyone who has had sexual relations without using a latex condom. We need to protect ourselves all the time, every time—not just some of the time.

Sarah used protection *almost* every time and that wasn't good enough. Just one unsafe sexual experience is enough.

I'll keep Sarah in my heart forever, but I'll also keep her in my mind to make sure I'm doing the right thing. Let Sarah be an example to every teenager. Believe me, it's very painful when you realize some sexual encounter that happened very long ago, maybe one that was not even significant enough for you to remember, can change your whole life.

UNSAFE SEX

Anonymous

The anonymous author of "Unsafe Sex" was born in Jamaica and came to New York in 1987 at the age of 15. She is a mother, college student, and an apprentice in a construction company. She also occasionally works as a personal care aide. Her interests include writing poetry, track and field, and cooking Caribbean cuisine. She lives in New York City.

Unsafe sex—what does that mean to me? It means AIDS.

I am a twenty-one-year-old college student who practices unsafe sex. Being a college student and a mother of one I consider myself very intelligent and smart. So why do I practice unsafe sex? Does it have to do with the fact that I am black? Does it have to do with the fact that I am a woman? Does it have to do with the fact that my parents are not good role models? Does it have to do with the fact that the man I am with gets more love from me than I get from myself? Or does it have to do with the fact that I am just careless and don't give a damn?

There is only one white adult who I can truly call my friend, she is the only person who will take the time to discuss matters with me, whatever they may be. She gives me her true opinion on everything. I can't honestly tell you of a black person who will take the time out to help me, and I don't open up to many white people, so maybe it does have something to do with the fact that I am black . . . . blacks and whites look at many things differently.

I was raised by my father, and for the many years that I lived with him I have seen him with so many women and having so many children with different mothers that I grew to accept the fact that this was all right. I did not have a mother to tell me that the first time I make love I should protect myself, and so I just kept on having unsafe sex.

Hearing about AIDS did not mean much to me concerning my lovemaking habits. Unsafe sex is something that I am used to and enjoy, so why change?

I am not sure if the fact that I am a woman has anything to do with my having unsafe sex. The way I see it is like this . . . women were always taught to try and please their men, do as their men ask. Even though times have changed some things remain the same. My man hates using condoms, and even though I am risking my life I do have unsafe sex with him. From the age of seventeen I have been living with this guy who was twenty years old at the time. Throughout our relationship I have discovered that my partner has been having other affairs and I still ended up having unsafe sex with him over and over again, I am just being careless and not giving a damn about killing myself.

Every day I think about the possibility that my partner and I might both have the HIV virus and not even know because I am so scared. And I think, what would I do and what would become of my son? The fact that I have been thinking about this AIDS issue so much has everything to do with the fact that I am only thinking and living for my son. Maybe if it wasn't for my son, I would not even give a second thought to AIDS because I love my man so much. When having sex with my man I don't give a second thought about the danger that we might both be facing. I just think about getting the best of what I am getting. After waking up and facing reality, I just push all the possibilities aside and just say to myself, "If he dies from AIDS, I will die with him, because I love him so much." It is so much easier for me to live with a separation by something that we both decide on, but for him to be taken away from me by death, I just don't know if I could go on.

Oh, but I am awake now, and just talking to my friend makes me realize how precious my life is and that I am on this planet to make a contribution. She made me realize how much my son needs me, and with tears coming from my eyes, she made me realize that it is time that I start thinking about myself and start doing something for me, because I am special. I'm going to take a step a *big* step, I am going to go and get tested and then take it from there. May God be with me.

SAVAGE GRACE

Mark Matousek

Mark Matousek is the author of a memoir, *Sex Death Enlightenment,* and co-author (with Andrew Harvey) of *Dialogues with a Modern Mystic.* Formerly Senior Editor of *Interview,* he has worked as an editor at *Newsweek* and has been a columnist for *Details* and *Harper's Bazaar.* Specializing in the journalism of consciousness, he is currently a contributing editor to *Common Boundary,* where his column, "The Naked Eye," appears six times a year. Matousek lives in New York City with his partner, Louis Morhaim.

> *When thought is obliged by an attack of physical pain, however slight, to recognize the presence of affliction, a state of mind is brought about, as acute as that of a condemned man who is forced to look for hours at the guillotine that is going to cut off his head. Human beings can live for twenty or fifty years in this acute state. We pass quite close to them without realizing it. What man is capable of discerning such souls unless Christ himself looks through his eyes?*
>
> —SIMONE WEIL

The night I became infected with HIV, there was a thunderstorm in the valley where I lived. I drove around my ex-lover's block, steering past trees stuck down by lightning, squinting through the rainy windshield, debating whether or not to knock on Bob's door for sex. I remember a feeling of danger—enhanced by the weather, I'm sure, and the nasty thrill of seducing a person you no longer love. After we'd finished our violent, sloppy encounter, I walked back into the downpour feeling spent and exhilarated.

Six years later, when Bob got sick, we talked about what AIDS was like. "You're not going to believe me, but I've never been happier in my life."

I studied his face for irony. "But you might die," I said.

"Worse things could happen." Bob was serious. Clearly something had shifted in him since his diagnosis. He was softer now, more circumspect. The mentor relationship we'd had since I was 18, when he, a successful show business mogul, plucked me from juvenile delinquency and showed me how to clean up my act, was finally becoming a friendship between equals. Without the trappings of movie-star clients and limousines, I was seeing my former hero for who he was, naked, accessible, human: AIDS had given Bob the exit he'd been waiting for from a fast-track life that bored him and permitted him to spend his days with the things he loved most: Schwartzkopf singing "The Four Last Songs," the Navajo art of R. C. Gorman.

Satisfying the needs of his soul, Bob had also been spurred by illness to explore the possibilities of spirit. Though a diehard atheist, he'd begun to think about his relationship to God, to investigate wisdom literature, to ask questions about the nature of existence. Much of this education was taking place under the tutelage of a newfound friend, death-and-dying pioneer Stephen Levine, whose many books were stacked on the nightstand. "It's like walking through the looking glass," Bob mused that afternoon. "Like falling down the rabbit hole and wondering which side is crazy, the flat old world or the wonderland. I'm not sure what I believe anymore, but it's all suddenly so fascinating. Awesome, in fact."

Two years after Bob died, I sat with Stephen and Ondrea Levine in a hotel room in New York City, talking about the epidemic. Stephen rolled a cigarette; next to him sat his bewitching wife, whose unlikely recoveries from cancer and lupus could put the chaplain at Lourdes to shame. They spoke about how much Bob, and people like him, were changing. "The truth is that nowhere on the planet—not in any ashram, monastery, or school—is spiritual awakening happening more rapidly than in the AIDS community," said Stephen, lighting up. "Nowhere do you find this enormity of heart, the dying nursing the dying, lovers burying lovers. It's completely extraordinary."

His remark has remained with me like a credo through the years, as I—and thousands like me—continue to "die by inches." While it's true that our lives have been shattered by HIV, it is also true that within this destruction, profound insights have occurred, deepening our vision, purpose, and faith. Knowing we may die very soon, we've been forced to look toward eternity, to treasure what we have; to realize, as a monk once wrote, that "if the cardinal's flight from bank to bank were less brief, it would also be less glorious."

Growth often accelerates in this intensified climate. With nothing left to lose, risk takes on new meaning. Challenges that were daunting before an HIV diagnosis seem like nothing compared to the prospect of dying without having done them. With old values falling away, many of us have made what seem like erratic, extreme movements in search of happiness and spiritual meaning. One friend left his career as a Wall Street attorney to meditate and chop vegetables in a Zen monastery; another gave up a successful arts career to run grief support groups and to train to be a therapist. A drug addict got sober, then, finding out that she was HIV-positive, became a national spokesperson for women with the virus.

Among those who have not been infected but work closely with the community, these changes have been equally inspiring.

A woman I interviewed left her home in the suburbs to nurse her son until his death from AIDS, then became ordained as an interfaith minister. A socialite and fashion designer abandoned her glittery life to fundraise for AIDS organizations, eventually opening her own nonprofit center in New York City. These personal revolutions, set in motion by tragedy, have heartened and reminded us that even in the worst of times, disaster can be used to draw us nearer together, to inspire us to become authentic, to open our hearts, and to seek enlightenment.

For me, the relationship between HIV and spiritual life has been equally fruitful and dramatic. It began on a trip to Jamaica in 1986. Having coffee with my best friend John in our hotel room, I discovered a purple spot on his foot that hadn't been there the day before. Five months later, panting behind an oxygen mask, John suffocated to death in a room overlooking an airshaft in Roosevelt Hospital. Knowing that my own funeral could be next, I panicked, not only for fear of dying, but also of realizing how ignorant I was in terms of my inner life. Quitting my vacuous career in publishing, I followed a mystical friend to Germany, where I met my spiritual teacher, Mother Meera, then continued on to India, where I took up the long-avoided challenge of writing fiction. Suddenly, everything was urgent, nothing could wait, and while this awareness of emergency created anxiety, it also brought my life into focus.

Returning to Manhattan deeply changed but forced to earn a living, I forewent limousine chasing for the journalism of consciousness. Although I had long assumed I was HIV-positive, and acted accordingly, it was not until 1989 that I finally surrendered to my new lover's insistence on taking the blood test. I'll never forget the look of pity on the technician's face as he read my results. I assured him that I was just fine. (I was more upset by my 24-year-old lover's positive test result than by my own.) But as the news sank in, I discovered that the transition from a shadow of doubt to confirmation was more significant than I'd anticipated: the leap, in essence, from dating to marriage. When this virus becomes a formal part of you, your identity shifts. In the same way that having a ring slipped on your finger serves to tie the knot, acknowledgment of HIV renders peaceful cohabitation with this strange bedfellow a necessary, everyday affair.

For me, this has been the ideal predicament: carrying a potentially fatal bug (with its urgent message not to waste time) while remaining outwardly unscathed. I've often said that AIDS has actually saved my life, propelling me to change, encouraging me to confront what's difficult, urging my fascination with things divine. There is nothing Pollyanna in this; it does not imply that I'd have chosen this virus, or that I would not cure it tomorrow if I could. But there have been undeniable benefits to having the myth of immortality exploded. Like thousands of others living in this limbo, I've founds depths and doors and potentials *in extremis* that I didn't now existed before. Forced to look beyond the body for metaphysical meaning, I've learned that within the horror lies a tremendous mystery.

Still, it's hard to be grateful for suffering. My feelings about AIDS are far more complex than gratitude can articulate. They have taken root in a realm beyond words, inspired by the awe at this fabulous pattern of death, grief, and regeneration, at watching yourself and others transcend terrors you thought would kill you. This intimacy with suffering puts you in a state like the one described by Hindu teacher and AIDS pioneer Ma Jaya Bhagavate of being in "complete agony and complete ecstasy" at the exact same moment.

Unfortunately, not everyone agrees about the honey in the rock. Due to my own transformative experience, and those that I've witnessed around me since the appearance of AIDS, I came to my research expecting others to agree with this perspective. I was wrong. In point of fact, 13 years into an epidemic that is only getting worse, the "S" word (spirituality) has come to have a surprisingly checkered reputation in the AIDS community. Speaking with People with AIDS (PWAs) and their lovers, therapists, doctors, ministers, authors, and gurus, it often seemed repugnant to discuss God in the midst of affliction, rather like rhapsodizing on My Lai.

"It's hard to say anything good about AIDS," admits Karen Ziegler, a minister who works with the Metropolitan Community Church in Manhattan, "I just want it to be over." Instigating conversations about spirituality in the presence of suffering, I learned, is to risk vulgarity, to miss the point, to literalize what is by its nature subtle, personal, and silent. As Joe Miller, a PWA living in New York, puts it, "Spirituality is like sex: The ones who really have it don't talk about it."

There are two primary reasons for resistance to the "S" word. The first concerns the attitude of organized religion toward homosexuals, who continue to dominate the AIDS community. Paul Monette, whose memoir *Borrowed Time* (about nursing his lover until his death) put AIDS on the literary map and whose *Becoming a Man* won the 1992 National Book Award for nonfiction, makes no bones about this ambivalence. "Organized religion is the world's worst problem," says Monette, who has lived with AIDS since 1989. "Fundamentalism the world over is why we've been genocided as a people." Karen Ziegler agrees. "Although gays have always been a spiritual people, many refuse to use the word because they've been so abused by the church. The fight against homosexuality in organized religion is the biggest [battle] in the church since the days of slavery. People talk about salvation, but for many of us, coming out is like salvation. Our presence through AIDS is challenging people who wouldn't have come to terms with their homophobia in any other way. That's what I call spiritual growth." Even within the Catholic Church, whose stand on AIDS remains questionable (the gay group Dignity was recently refused communion in Los Angeles, then taken in by the Episcopalians), inroads have begun to be made, with church-run hospices functioning in San Francisco and other urban areas.

Still, the sheer magnitude of AIDS and all the attendant issues are enough to turn some former believers into skeptics. John McIlveen, who heads the volunteer division of the PWA Coalition in New York, is one of them. "My faith has dwindled during the AIDS crisis," admits this former Catholic. "It's left me more existential." A blue-eyed all-American of 33, McIlveen has not been infected but lives with an HIV-positive lover. The shadow of death weighs heavily. "The serial loss is devastating. I've watched at least a dozen volunteers die in the past two years. I ask myself, if there's a God, why is this happening? This whole tragedy has made me cynical."

This cynicism has only been strengthened by certain factions of the New Age movement, whose saccharine philosophy is the second major obstacle to spirit among individuals groping with the gritty reality of AIDS. Responding to cries of helplessness and fatality following the first diagnoses in the early 1980s, the psychological pendulum swung to the opposite extreme in an effort to rally people away from victimhood toward the possibilities of self-healing and survival. Foremost among this group of advocates was Louise Hay, a Science of Mind minister whose books (including *You Can Heal Your Own Life*) have sold in the millions and whose name has become synonymous with pop notions of self-created reality and "taking responsibility" for illness.

Beginning in 1985, Hay (who refused to be interviewed for this piece) formed the first of many AIDS healing circles across the country, urging the six men in her living room to drop their self-pity and take charge, using affirmations, visualizations, mirror work, teddy bears, and other devices aimed at fostering self-love and its supposed correlate, spontaneous physical healing.

Proffering what Paul Monette dubs "Readers Digest psychology," with its simplistic think-happy-get-healthy message, Hay seemed to offer a sunny alternative to slow and painful death. Those at risk, and those already dying, flocked to self-empowerment's ray of hope, following the injunction to uproot their evil death wish by becoming vigilantes of negativism.

This philosophy's dangerous fallout has struck many, including myself. Working as a volunteer at New York's Cabrini Hospice, I was spoon-feeding a very sick patient one day when a member of the New York Healing Circle came by for a visit. "I always knew he was a negative person," this fellow said to me afterward in the hall, referring to the man in bed. Asked why I was wearing a mask in the room, I informed him that our patient had active TB. He laughed at my self-protective precaution. "But no one can give you anything you don't want!" he scoffed.

Years later, in a more sophisticated fashion, Marianne Williamson gained enormous popularity using a channeled Christian text called *A Course in Miracles* to promulgate a similar outwit-the-darkness thesis, leading many, through misinterpretation and oversimplification, into a philosophical quagmire. Though nominally nonjudgmental, the *Course,* like Hay's Science of Mind, may set the seeker up for a fall with its fierce emphasis on positive thinking. "There's this underlying sense of right and wrong," says Cynthia O'Neal, a prominent spokesperson for the AIDS community who helped Williamson found the Manhattan Center for Living. "There's an enormous difference between being responsible for your illness and being responsible to it, doing everything in your power to help yourself heal and so on. With the former, self-blame is almost inevitable," claims O'Neal, who left the fold two years ago to form her own nonprofit center, Friends in Deed.

"It's all a little too flip," says Eric Schneider, a gestalt therapist and martial arts instructor who works with a largely HIV-affected clientele in New York City. "I spend a lot of time with people deconstructing ideas from Louise and Marianne. Without guidance, you can go very far down a wrong path."

These failures can't be pinned solely on these New Age messengers, however. "It wasn't entirely their fault," admits Sally Fisher, a former acting coach who founded the AIDS Mastery workshop seven years ago. "In the beginning, there was a misunderstanding about the parthenogenesis of the disease. People thought they were keeping AIDS away with affirmations, but actually it was just what we now refer to as the "honeymoon period.'"

Having already nursed a son through adolescent Hodgkin's disease, Fisher was no stranger to hospital rooms when theater friends, diagnosed with AIDS, urged her to "get off her ass and do something useful." Adapting her performance skills to the need for expression and truth-telling incumbent on people facing death, Fisher soon discovered that her own nuts-and-bolts behavioral approach to healing was at odds with the idealistic spoutings of others. "The New Age became another kind of fundamentalism, a storehouse of magical thinking for people in search of a magic bullet. Unfortunately, when they finally did get sick, they blamed themselves for doing something wrong."

Thus many infected and dying individuals, alienated by both the religious and New Age contingents, found themselves in no-man's land, compelled to create an approach to healing and spirituality forged from their own experience, meeting their own particular needs, incorporating their own unique gifts, and drawing from the best of mainstream and alternative sources. "There are a million possibilities between death and denial," says Sally Fisher. "We just had to find them."

Moving into this realm of possibility, the first thing that becomes obvious is the crucial role that solidarity, revolt, and imagination have played in the AIDS movement. Hitting a marginalized population "already high in survival skills" (according to Schneider) and eager for their civil rights, the epidemic has acted as a social powderkeg, unleashing astounding powers of resourcefulness and community support, an alembic in which activism and spirituality are distilled and linked.

Witness the facts. In 1983, two years after the first cases of Gay Related Immune Deficiency (GRID) were diagnosed, 45 community-based organizations had formed around the country. By 1990, this network had snowballed to nearly 800 groups (with services including legal aid; alternative health care; political advocacy; and every manner of medical, psychological, and pastoral support), organized to meet the needs of people affected by HIV and the individuals around them. This explosion of *caritas* has been fueled by desperation and the growing realization that, as outsiders in a right-wing era, this community would have to care for itself or suffer even more deeply. According to sociologist Susan Chambre, volunteers offered their services in droves as a "way to cope with the uncertainties and ambiguities of the epidemic, as well as a way to bear witness" to this unexpected tragedy. Among these groups, many, such as New York's PWA Coalition (where 75 percent of the volunteers are living with AIDS) were instigated by people with AIDS themselves. "Again and again, we've seen the dying cross the wound to help their brothers," observes Stephen Levine. "First you're outcast by society and then you're told you might die!" adds Sally Fisher. "This group, which had been legislated against and vilified, had to find a way to nourish itself in the face of disaster."

Anger has been one tool that, when used skillfully, has accelerated self-actualization as well as shifted the balance in social power. Many have turned to civil disobedience to protest medical, political, and legal injustices and have found it to be a vehicle for both empowerment and the release of hostility bred from oppression. "Social consciousness is crucial to everyone in a beleaguered world," Paul Monette told me in February, en route to deliver a scathing speech before the Library of Congress in Washington. "By taking anger away from people, some forms of spirituality keep people from becoming part of the political battle. Anger against injustice is the most significant emotion an adult can feel."

Inspiring as anger may be, however, it is only one piece of the healing puzzle. "It may help change laws, but if it helps their lovers dying in bed, I don't know," says Stephen Levine. "There's a need to find something to sustain yourself in the face of death that goes deeper than rage," adds Fisher.

Determined to be active martyrs instead of helpless victims, many PWAs are working hard to locate this middle path between rage and compassion. Their drive to transform personal suffering into public good is mythic in texture. According to Paul Bellman, a Manhattan internist whose practice is largely devoted to people living with HIV, "People with AIDS are the real heroes of our time, even more than those suffering from other diseases. Being young, many people with HIV embark on a kind of medical, psychological, and spiritual quest to find better treatments and discover themselves. It becomes a hero's journey."

Ten years ago, Dean Rolston was a high-powered Wall Street attorney art world maven, and part-time Zen student, up to his eyebrows in New York City hysteria and longing for a break. An urbane man of 40, renowned on two coasts for his remarkable wit and trademark headscarf, Rolston grew tired of elbowing the best and brightest, and used AIDS as an exit from a world he'd outgrown. "This illness gave me permission to change," emphasizes Rolston, who ditched Manhattan for the serenity of the Green Gulch monastery outside of San Francisco following his diagnosis in 1987.

This change of scenery has had unexpected rewards, both

spiritual and medical. Like an increasing number of PWAs, Rolston has continued to outlive his physicians' prognoses for survival ("It's almost embarrassing," he laughs), attributing his continued relatively good health to changes of life-style and priorities.

Living with AIDS, he claims, has radically transformed his character. "You become more tender and expressive as you pierce the veil of ordinary reality and seek deeper things," says Rolston, who now channels his professional savvy into writing (HarperSanFrancisco is planning to publish his AIDS memoir in 1994), and curating art shows for charitable organizations, such as the San Francisco Zen Hospice. Often this tenderness leads to unexpected spiritual insights. During a recent brush with death, Rolston reports an experience of *satori* (enlightenment) that took him to "a completely different level of reality, a buoyancy lighter than air. You begin to realize that everything is perfect around you, pleasant and unpleasant," he explains with a characteristic mix of amusement and dispassion. "Even the things you dread become fascinating."

In this heightened state, the sacredness of everyday life often becomes more vivid. "The truth is, there are Buddhas everywhere!" Rolston laughs. "It's astonishing where you run into them—in the glowing eyes of a boy on the bus, in the Cockney nurse sticking needles in your arm." What's more, it doesn't necessarily take sitting on a zafu to realize this. "Dying is very intense spiritual practice, if you're paying attention," notes Rolston. "Formal practice begins to seem redundant." For other people with AIDS, the inverse holds true. According to Dr. Rick Levine, a number of patients at the Maitri Hospice with no meditation background have taken up rigorous practice and been ordained as Buddhist monks in their last months of life.

Although the experience of deepened spirituality seems to be nearly universal among those touched by AIDS, many who call themselves atheists prefer to clothe their epiphanies in humanist terms. "My faith is in those I love and trust," says John McIlveen, who finds inspiration in "the charity of other people." Paul Monette, an ex-Episcopalian who continues to take communion, feels similarly, citing the "exquisite examples of people living out their love" as God enough.

This feeling of brotherhood is the spiritual bridge for many who are put off by religious language. Moved by a sense of kinship with, and responsibility toward, those who have died before him, New York *Times* deputy editor Jeffrey Schmalz was the first reporter to come out in print about his disease. He has used his situation to increase sorely needed, sensitive AIDS coverage in the mainstream media, and has even raised the issue of spirituality concerning the epidemic. In an editorial last year, Schmalz described a sudden urge to go to church before having surgery on an irreversible brain condition. Claiming that it would be "hypocritical to turn to God in a moment of desperation," Schmalz was amazed by the flood of letters (and Bibles) that arrived after the article appeared. "People wrote to say that crisis is exactly when one should turn to God," Schmalz tells me in the newsroom. "This is not to say that when my time comes, I won't be a hypocrite. There's an old saying that there are no atheists in foxholes," he says with a smile.

While holding to his skepticism, Schmalz sees that mortal illness cannot help but instigate existential questions. "AIDS has forced me to rethink all this rather dramatically, which is a spiritual happening in itself." In the meantime, his inspiration comes from the dead, whose cause he continues to champion. "As the end approaches, my friends who've gone seem very close," says Schmalz. "They're my conscience and my cheering section, urging me on, giving me strength. When I get very tired, they say to me, 'Not yet, Jeff, keep going.'"

While it would appear that such inspiration is a welcome

addition to character, referring to AIDS as a benefit causes a knee-jerk reaction in almost everyone. "When people say that HIV's a gift, it takes for granted all the other gifts we're given every moment. That pisses me off!" says Eric Schneider. Even the faithful find themselves bemused. "I'll tell you, honey, this disease is a blessing I could live without!" says Phyllis Marks, stroking the head of her Maltese sidekick, Susie. A sexy woman of 50 dressed in skin-tight jeans and cowboy boots, Marks has known she is HIV-positive since 1986. Though ironic about this equivocal gift, she admits that the wakeup call came just in time. "I needed an excuse to turn things around," claims Marks, echoing Dean Rolston. "I'd been searching all my life through drugs. Even though the process started with my getting sober, AIDS is what finally brought me to my knees."

"I can vouch for that," says her lover, Leila Gastil. Following Phyllis's diagnosis with AIDS-related lymphoma in 1991, the couple began a year-long practice of heart meditation with a Tibetan monk in New York. "In crisis, your powerlessness forces you constantly to turn to God," says Gastil. "For me, that has become the most comfortable place to live, with or without the disease. This community understands and supports that."

This support offers tangible results. "When you have AIDS, the concepts of home and family become crucial," admits Marks, who has called on the community in darkest times. "Whenever I've had a major treatment—spinal taps, bone marrow transplants, chemotherapy—I've asked people to pray for me. The amazing thing is that I never experienced any pain whatsoever when there was unified prayer. Knowing that people were sending me their love took the pain away. That was an extraordinary spiritual lesson," concludes Marks, whose cancer is now in remission.

Behind the army of individuals with AIDS is a sizable reserve of equally devoted but uninfected helpers, religious and secular, who have taken on the full-time job of helping people with AIDS bear their burden. Far from being martyrs, those that serve know that they're receiving as much as they give through the formidable opportunities for compassion that AIDS presents.

"It's an incredible privilege to be invited to share a person's death," says Ma Jaya Bhagavate, whose remarkable work in this community has distinguished her among American religious figures since the beginning of the epidemic. In addition to founding a score of charitable organizations around the country, Ma Jaya regularly visits hospitals and children's homes in Florida where her ashram is located, and around the country. Born in Brooklyn, this Hindu teacher is loved for a gutsy, flamboyant style that calls everyone into the fray. "Whoever falls into my arms, I hold," says Ma Jaya in her Coney Island accent. "I juice them up so they don't die dry. If spiritual teachers would get into the trenches and kiss these people's brows and lesions, they'd see that you don't have to preach about God. You just gotta be ready with a God answer."

Ma Jaya counsels devotees with AIDS to keep on giving till they drop. "You think I let my gay men die in peace?" she says. "Hell, no. They work their butts off." In the process, she reminds them always of the blessing of service. "You gotta remember that when you're witnessing somebody's death, you're a guest," she insists. "That honor must be respected."

Cynthia O'Neal understands this privilege well. Married and the mother of two grown sons, O'Neal was already on a spiritual path when her colleagues in show business began coming down with AIDS. Looking for ways to cope with her grief, this graceful ex-model found her way to a Louise Hay workshop, and there had an experience that changed her philosophical and professional life.

"There was a young man asleep on the floor next to me," she remembers, as we sit on a sofa at Friends in Deed, the plush, lower-Manhattan center O'Neal founded with Oscar-winning director Mike Nichols. "He was pale and thin, obviously ill, and without knowing why, I suddenly picked him up and put him in my lap. He opened his eyes, smiled, and went back to sleep. Later, Archie—that was his name—told the group that the hardest thing about having AIDS was the fear of letting everybody down. At the break I told him that I'd love to be his friend and that if he needed to die, it would be fine with me.

"Archie lived another year; then one day he elected to stop all treatment. His body was worn out, but spiritually he was just fine. The night he passed away, Archie, his lover, and I were all hugging on the bed. The room was candlelit; chamber music was playing. It was so exquisite, like a birth. This experience completely allayed my own fears about dying. Archie taught me how to die."

Lyrical as this sounds, O'Neal admits that not everyone is so lucky. "People die the way they lived," she says. Recognizing this, therapists such as Eric Schneider use their practice to focus as much on the psychological and spiritual surrounding HIV as on the virus itself. "The thrust of my work is that—since none of us are getting out of this alive—HIV doesn't matter much," says Schneider, sucking on a pipe in his Chelsea office. "At root, these aren't AIDS experiences, they're human experiences." But working with individuals whose life expectancy may be curtailed alters the intensity of the therapeutic process. "In terms of self-actualization, many people with this disease are on the fast track, which makes me speed up the work." This sense of urgency creates commensurate opportunity. "If I'm teaching aikido, and push someone beyond his limits, he will tap into a deeper resource. Emergency causes us to access something that transcends the usual ways we organize our lives."

Many of us living with HIV and AIDS are making concerted efforts to integrate psychospiritual healing with the physical realities of immune deficiency. Called upon to reimagine a condition deemed incurable by the mainstream medical establishment (but, in the light of growing numbers of long-term survivors, perhaps not so), we rely upon physicians (as well as therapists) who are willing to support us in our struggle to cultivate hope during this twilight period of pessimism and uncertainty.

"Most people living with HIV are relatively healthy," notes Dr. Bellman, adding that he believes AIDS will ultimately be shown to be a "curable disease." Alan Pressman, a veteran chiropractor and longtime advocate of alternative approaches to healing AIDS, agrees. "While accepting the biological component as an absolute necessity, people with HIV are going far beyond that, more than any group I've ever seen," says Pressman. "Nearly 100 percent of my clients are involved in more than just a biological approach to their illness." "We need to encourage the patient's search throughout this process," Bellman adds, "to look at it creatively and to support both body and soul in the healing journey."

One emotional aspect to consider has to do with feeling the sobering powers of grief. "Grief drives us to seek understanding and unity," explains Stephen Levine. "There may be nothing beautiful in suffering, but in the opening to pain something profound can come about. Unfortunately, brokenhearted America doesn't know how to grieve. Temples should be built for this purpose alone, sanctuaries for loss and weeping. The truth is that in 1993, in a world of such indifference and hostility, we don't need some fancy spirituality. If we could touch our pain with mercy, this would be Eden."

Ma Jaya emphatically agrees. "People have forgotten that death has a heart," she says. "You just gotta stop and listen."

Yesterday I went for my three-month checkup. On route, I picked up the New York *Times* and saw a picture of the Pope blessing a child with AIDS in Uganda. The caption noted that despite the fact that Uganda has the highest number of AIDS cases in Africa (over a million infected in this half-Catholic country), the Vatican continues to claim "chastity as the only defense" against the spread of HIV.

At the clinic, my doctor looks happy. He approves of my latest lab results; he is pleased by the numbers and ratios. My T-cells, whatever those are, seem to be normal. I'm not in immediate danger.

I leave the office feeling smug, not quite grateful enough (it seems to me) for continued good health as my friends get sicker. At home, an invitation has arrived, announcing the baptism of my best friend Carole's granddaughter. Carole, whose rosary hangs by my desk, was an ardent Catholic who died of AIDS last year after being infected during the only one-night stand of her life. Here was the granddaughter (named for her) she dreamt about but didn't live to see. I RSVP in her stead.

In an ironic passage, Aristotle defined luck as the moment the arrow hits the guy next to you. This is cold comfort, as the "worried well" and anyone dealing with survivors' guilt can testify. A faction of seronegative extremists actually claim to want HIV for solidarity. I've never been that crazy (my train will take off soon enough), but I do admit to feeling resigned sometimes: surreal, split off, already dead. So many have already left the station; death is no longer a surprise. Sometimes it doesn't even hurt.

Once a father approached a Buddhist master and asked how he could possibly bear to live in a world where he could not protect his children from annihilation. The master picked up a crystal goblet. "I like this glass," he said. "It makes a lovely sound when you flick it, and everything tastes more delicious when poured from its delicate shape. But when a wind comes along and shatters it into a thousand pieces, I won't be surprised. You see, I know the glass is already broken."

Is this spirituality? Perhaps. Writing this story, I came to question the implications of that word more than I had before. It seems to imply some separateness, some privilege, some otherness that may not be useful. Is it spiritual, or simply wise, to admit you're already broken? Thanks to HIV, I have come to live with this fact completely. Every morning the routine's the same. I open my eyes, check my armpits for lumps, the sheets for perspiration. I search my body in the shower for purple lesions, then inspect my tongue in the mirror for signs of thrush. At first these rituals were disturbing. Now they simply keep me on my toes.

The funniest thing about it is that I've grown to love this way of life—the intensity, clarity, poignancy—the ability to see things at their value, to measure life, at last, by its true and terminal standard. I laugh louder these days and cry at nothing. I work until my fingers hurt and I exercise my heart in love. The future is a fantasy and I think almost nothing about the past.

Of course, AIDS is terrible—a sentence to the guillotine. But terror can enlighten. Affliction has its gifts. Rainer Maria Rilke, who refused medication during his excruciating final illness, described this in a letter to a patroness. "It is true," wrote the poet, "that these mysteries are dreadful, and people have always drawn away from them. But where can we find anything sweet and glorious that would never wear this mask of the dreadful? Whoever does not, sometime or other, give his full and joyous consent to the dreadfulness of life, can never take possession of the unutterable abundance and power of our existence; can only walk on its edge, and one day, when the judgment is given, will have been neither alive nor dead."

This bitter wisdom cuts to the bone and reminds me of visiting an Italian artist years ago in his studio, He was in the process of restoring a neglected painting from the days of Michelangelo. Fascinated, I watched him dip a brush in a tin of stinking, acidic solution, then slide it across the encrusted canvas. Magically, an eye appeared through the grime, then the face of a smiling Madonna. Soon, the full pieta shone through, bathed in acrid-smelling tonic.

Our veils need dissolving too, else we miss the picture. Without a burn, a taste of death, we are strangers to the mystery. Shrouded by fear, we are blind to the fact that God makes seeds out of rolling heads.

ALL OF US
ARE LEAVING

Eve Ensler

Eve Ensler has been a playwright and screenwriter for more than ten years. Her plays include *The Depot, Ladies, Lemonade,* and *Reef and Particle.* Since 1982, Ms. Ensler has edited *Central Park,* a New York City journal of the arts and social theory. She was named to the Mayor's Commission on the Status of Women in 1983 and since then has become a founding member of several community-based organizations, including Women Helping Women and Anonymous Women for Peace and Candu. Ms. Ensler also teaches creative writing at New York University.

Every morning at 5 A.M. Sheila puts bitter melon herbal treatment in her rear end.

Mark is not worrying about caffeine.

Paul feels relieved by the catheter.

Tim is gaining weight.

They were sitting in the candlelight. My friends.
Around my kitchen table.

•

Mark visits the Divine Mother. She holds his head in silence and he has no self-pity.

Sheila lives with her mother for years but doesn't tell her about the virus because her mother's a crack addict and it would upset her.

Paul feels like a fish. His peripheral eyesight is gone and he can only swim straight ahead. His legs are fins. The branches from the city streets keep bumping into him.

Tim is a powerful city councilperson and he uses the word condom every chance he gets.

Sheila bought a big winter coat because the cold air is plutonium. It gets through everything.

Mark's body is sculpted and lean. When he wears white, the angels keep flying out of him.

The floor of Paul's studio apartment is the Hudson River. The hypodermic needles, medication packets and junk food wrappers have washed up on it.

Sheila's face is a brown inspiration. When she teaches in the ghetto school, the kids think she's pregnant because the fibroid tumors are so swollen inside her.

AZT. DDI. CMV. Can't we just try it.

Paul remembers dark dirty sex on his linoleum floor. He hasn't touched another body since he was diagnosed HIV. He craves sex the way foreigners crave their original language.

·

Tim makes his boyfriends leave when they look too deeply at him. He has many appointments and is only attached to the telephone.

Paul has another transfusion. He vomits right after the new blood comes in.

Toxic/Macrobiotic. Just eat the pudding.

Mark brings an African violet. He needs to talk after sex about his feelings and is tortured by his lover's silence.

Sheila's only told two people in seven years. She does not go out. People think she's angry at them or bitter about her career. When she used to sing you could hear the wind blow on the island.

Tim dreams about running for president, but he gets caught having anal sex with a Communist.

Paul wakes up and the medication is all gone from the bag. He thinks he's in the ocean and he's gasping for air. He can't remember why his mother isn't there.

Mark was told by his mother that everything has to do with his penis, the size of it mainly and the intention.

It should never have come to this.
Inside my blood.
At my table.

Tim is running . . . for another . . . term.

Mark is not afraid.

Paul is screaming about the triangles of sight that disappear without warning.

Sheila is inside sleeping.

T-CELLS. FALLING. BITTER MELON REMEDY.

Paul craves sherbet. It soothes the thrush.

Mark isn't worried about caffeine.

Tim eats McDonald's on the run.

Sheila eats only grains and greens.

No one is losing weight.

No one has PCP.

COLD SORES.

I would have held you then.

Mark goes to the gym. He keeps pumping and looking, looking and pumping.

Paul can't get out of the tub.

Sheila's T-CELLS are climbing.

Tim has lost his voice again from shouting.

·

Paul gets another transfusion. Then all his friends buy him a TV and VCR and he gets excited by "I Love Lucy."

Mark is talking about the soul. He is talking about the miracle everyone's searching for that's already here.

HIV is not an identity.

T-CELLS are not the only measure of inevitability.

We keep counting.

Paul is loudly quoting Chekhov.

Tim is angry in front of City Hall. He is throwing sticky purple condoms but he'd like to be throwing boulders.

Sheila dreams that she's been asked to give a solo piano concert. As she plays she sweats buckets of water which turns to blood which turns to something that looks like Thanksgiving gravy. Then when the people in tuxedos are trying to move away, Sheila realizes it's all her shit, her whole life of it, and she's happy suddenly, floating ducks and boats and wooden things on it.

Mark doesn't dream anymore. When he closes his eyes, yellow white light surrounds his heart and penis. He laughs when he feels the creator's hand on him. He laughs like he did once before, before he was seven, before his father left him.

Because they craved connection.

Because they longed to be touched.

•

Tim is getting handcuffed by a big man wearing rubber medical gloves. "Thank you for protecting me," he says, smiling sexy at the cop like he's about to give him head.

Paul calls me on the phone. His voice is breaking. He asks me with a newborn need if I'll come right over.

In a letter Mark recently wrote me, "I am monstrously impatient inside, full of rage at the incapacity to go deeply enough, passionately enough."

Those that fucked the hardest were in search of it.

Tim is waving from the paddy wagon to his constituents. He notices his cheek is bleeding and tries to cover it.

The virus is passed through semen, blood, and mother's milk. The virus is passed through us.

A huge herb pill is stuck in Sheila's throat. She imagines choking and never coming out of it. And dying and never singing. She got it when she went back to him for one night after seven years. Choking because it stuck in her. Never singing. Throat. Because he was safe, she thought. He was her husband. He was familiar.

I hold Paul and his head is banging my shoulder as the big sea fish tears rock out of him. I am the midwife, birthing him into the reality of his death. His denial is the placenta that afterwards passes through me.

Is it as devastating as it seems or is it because I know them?

·

Around my table. Inside my house.

I force Sheila to stay for tea.

I give Tim some more bean salad.

I bring Paul Fig Newtons.

Mark is eating from the pan.

Mark is eating from the sky, devouring stars, swallowing night.

Sheila is howling at the streetlight that could have been the moon.

Tim is trying to get the others through.

Paul is wearing Chinese slippers and they are damp from where his fins are leaking.

All of us are counting now.

All of us are leaving.

JIMMY PARKER
and
JEAN LECHANCE

———————— · ————————

Tom Phillips

Tom Phillips writes, "I presently work as a case worker in an innovative Boston AIDS organization called the Justice Resource Institute, helping PWAs find federal housing subsidy. Before this post, I worked for nearly nine years in Boston's homeless world, first in the city's largest shelter and then at a drop-in center/soup kitchen. I had some involvement in the housing of hundreds of homeless men and women, and it was during this period that I wrote the following pieces—just two snapshots of homeless PWAs I befriended, drove around, listened to, moved furniture with, and completed bureaucratic forms for before they perished."

JIMMY PARKER

Just received word from Annie Lewis that Jimmy Lewis (actually Jimmy Parker), her son by her first marriage, died in his sleep Friday of AIDS. He was 38 years old, glad to have a loving mother, his own apartment to kick his feet up in, and was after me for weeks to find him a free frying pan from a freebee warehouse. I had been driving around for weeks with a fucking frying pan in my trunk hoping to run into Jimmy. I would have given it to him last I saw him—at Boston City Hospital in the registration I.D. card line; but he was in a fit of frustration over needing to wait in the line although he was only at the hospital to have his prescription renewed for the hundredth time.

All there is left of Jimmy is that skillet reminder and the persistent memory of his lithe comebacking silhouette, sailor's cap atop, skimming the dawn sidewalk. I'd always seen him leaving the methadone clinic at dawn when I'd be arriving at work. Him moving like a purposeful bug past the all-night whores and two-bit pimps at the frenetic pace only addicts know and me moving like a slow and dull bear.

JEAN LECHANCE

Death, death . . . more death. Everywhere like a foul fog that keeps blowing in, hogging up the landscape just after a clearing's made us feel clean again inside.

This time—Jean LeChance, found five days' perished in his roominghouse room alone and still finally. No more fistfuls of blank housing applications he'd mostly fill out independently, finally too crumpled and irrelevant with his shopping bags of verifications, identifications, validations, and still more applications for still more mailing lists. Jean was a paper freak, loved documenting documents, ready to prove who helped him and who was part of that force that kept him striving and running and shrieking at statues in the churchyard, or flinging chairs in a shelter line, or freaking out violently in a V.A. clinic.

The virus took his mind like a violent and sudden robbery.

Jean was a poet full of mystery, effete with elegance, delicate as if you could see him walking a dog or reading to kids, ever-repentent to his wheelchair Cajun mother who sent him North thirty years hence for education.

She thinks it best now Jean come back home to New Orleans like his last ten shelter years were a wayward odyssey, a trip only as hellish as Jean would divulge. Tomorrow begins the battle of finding an undertaker with profit on the back burner who'll help walk the welfare funeral fund maze to send Jean home with his education intact.

ONE MOTHER'S STORY

Anonymous

The anonymous author of "One Mother's Story" writes, "Living this experience causes much inner conflict. Placing my feelings on paper enables me to picture my situation differently—mother and daughter apart, yet a definitive togetherness, in life, in death."

I am sixty years old. I have a B.A. degree in sociology, and I'm working on a master's degree and writing a thesis, a documentary on learning disabilities.

I have decided to put on paper some of the heartfelt issues concerning my daughter who passed this life in the summer of 1993. She died of AIDS. I am a mother of two children; with my daughter passing I have one son. My daughter gave birth to four children, and I have been instrumental in raising all of her children, most of their lives.

My daughter decided to leave my home when she was seenteen years old. I had just moved into a beautiful four-room apartment, newly furnished, and was expecting many happy days ahead. Just to backtrack a little: I raised my daughter as a single parent, from the tender age of less than a year old. She died at the age of thirty-seven. I think it is important to say at this time that raising girl-children as a single parent causes many unforeseen problems, sometimes, in their future relationships.

My daughter never came to grips with the missing male figure. I raised her with the distinct objective of trying to be mother and father as best I could. I dressed her well. I kept food on the table. I worked. I worked. I worked.

My background: I finished high school and worked in the garment district, in the famous downtown section in New York, Thirty-third Street. "Piece workers" was our title in the factory. I made two cents a garment, and made a large enough salary to pay rent, take care of an ailing mother, and keep myself going.

My daughter developed a hard shell as life went on. She couldn't really relate to men. She felt cheated and left-out of life. I sent her to the best schools. She finished high school and went on to a business institute, became a Columbia University secretary. She still wasn't happy. My daughter married twice and divorced twice.

Needless to say, when you are a mother of an addicted child with AIDS, you wonder: where did you go wrong? She finally confessed that she couldn't live without drugs. She became an avid follower of drug people. She went to drug programs and fell off the wagon time and time again. Eventually I became part of a volunteer drug counseling program and listened to other addicted women who'd left their children with their parents. And I learned that all women with drug problems and children regret the way they depend on and abuse their mothers with their dependency. I became a more compassionate mother to my daughter when I realized she was not against me personally. But she had needs that superceded the normal love you give a daughter. I had to preserve her life with my love or else lose her to suicide or worse.

Eventually, she moved from the Bronx to Brooklyn to

Manhattan to Queens. I hardly ever knew where she was. She somehow was determined not to come home unless she was destitute and strung out. Thank God I had Jesus. I know that my faith in God brought me through.

One day she called me from New Jersey and told me the terrible things she was going through. I begged her to come home to me. I told her I would take care of her. She said no. I prayed and prayed. Then one day she called and said, "I know you're praying, Mama. Come and get me."

I ordered a van to go to Jersey in zero-degree weather. Just breathing was like taking in icicles. When I got there she was lying on a couch in a haze of cigarette smoke and whatever else included. I picked her up, put her stuff in the van, and brought her to my house.

Unfortunately, my daughter, in her addiction, was not comfortable in a stable environment. She soon became a part of the homeless population, eating out of church programs, sleeping in shelters, and hating every moment. In between these homeless jaunts she would come to me with large bags of clothes, and it seemed she traveled from place to place, like a bag lady, she carried her belongings on her person. When she would say goodbye to me (after staying as long as she would allow herself to keep still) my heart would go out the door with her, for I never knew what den or dive or on what subway bench she would find herself. It's one thing to see a boy-child live like this, but when a mother watches her girl-child ravaged and addicted and hunted down like an animal, this is not describable.

She would tell me that there was a contract out on her life. She could not walk down certain streets because she had enemies in the drug scene looking for her. I prayed she wouldn't get killed like many of the women I knew who were shot and killed by their pimps and those who put them out on the street. This was not a TV show I was thrown into. This was my child who I gave birth to.

I watched my 130–pound daughter go down to 75 or 80 pounds. I sat by her bedside and watched her vomit buckets of black blood. She developed a brain tumor, bleeding on the brain, pancreatic disease, trouble in the abdomen, numerous other viruses, bleeding ulcers, teeth that could not chew but just suck liquids, poor sight, double kidney failure. Dialysis collapsed every vital artery, and when there was no place left, she received daily dialysis through her groin. Her emaciated body was almost purple. My child who had beautiful skin and dressed like she was born in Paris.

The last four months of my daughter's life was spent in a hospital in Manhattan. Before she passed, we formed a bond and she cried and thanked me for giving her children a real chance to be raised as she was raised. Before this, she would always criticize me for instilling religious and moral values in her life. After suffering, she realized it was the faith in God that I told her about that helped her endure the self-destruction she placed on herself by going back on drugs, even on dialysis. The drugs kept her from saying thank you, Mom, for raising my four kids, from babies to six, thirteen, fifteen, nineteen.

She finally said, "I love you, Mommy. Forgive me for not realizing in your old age you gave your life to my four kids. I can't take the credit for how beautiful they've turned out because many times I have been out of it. But I'm so proud of my children. Look how big they are." She asked God to forgive her rebellious spirit. God is love. I believe He hears all sincere prayers. My daughter is a picture of life's other side.

It has only been eight months since her death. I didn't think I could even write this much on paper. However, when I was asked, I said as a mother I would contribute to the understanding of how a mother copes with this type of unfortunate situation. I want the world to know there is no bitterness in my heart about this experience. I had to learn the hard way. There are mountains to climb in this life: highs and lows. But there is a

God who weighs and balances our life checkbooks. I am a survivor with a testimony.

I love you, my daughter in life and in death. I hope you have finally found eternal rest.

Your Mother Forever

MY FAVORITE UNCLE IS HIV-POSITIVE

Akia Thomas

Akia Thomas is a student at Springfield Gardens High School in Queens, New York.

I always knew there was something quite different about my uncle. When I was little, I even wondered how he could be an uncle at all when, to my eyes, he acted and looked just like a woman. My uncle would spend a long time in the mirror doing his hair, plucking his eyebrows, putting different facial creams on his face and shaping his lips with lipliner—things I considered feminine. I even remember asking him why he never wore a skirt like other women.

It wasn't until I was around six that I realized that my uncle really was a man. A couple of years later I figured out that one of the things that was different about him was that he liked other men. I would wonder why he and his male friends acted like a man and a woman do—not sexually but just in terms of the closeness that they had with each other.

The fact that my uncle is gay never upset me because in my family it was always accepted. If anything, my uncle's being gay has helped me. Every time I am having guy problems, he's the one I go to for advice because I know he'll understand.

I think I cherish our relationship so much because, out of all my family, my uncle is the only one who understands what it is like to be a teenager. In some ways he is still like a teenager himself. My uncle has a different attitude on life than most adults. Unlike my "boring" parents, he has never settled down. He hangs out with his friends just like I do. He still goes out to clubs and parties till all times of the night. I've heard the saying "gay people have more fun" and, at least in my uncle's case, that's true.

He also has a crazy sense of humor. If you do something stupid like I tend to do, he makes sure everybody in the family hears about it over and over again. My father is his favorite target. He's the oldest brother and my uncle loves to talk about how old he acts. He is always telling me, "Your father is jealous of me because he's old and bitter and I am young and lovely." In spite of the jokes, their relationship is very close.

My uncle doesn't just keep me entertained, he also listens to my problems and gives me advice when I need it. For instance, this past summer I was seeing this guy and my parents didn't like it because he was six years older than me. My mother stopped trusting me even though she didn't have a reason to and my father treated me like a child who was unable to have her own life. It was the worst time of my life because it seemed as though my family had turned against me.

The only person I could talk to was my uncle. I told him all about the guy, things I didn't tell anybody else. I asked him if I should continue to see him or call it quits because my family disapproved of our friendship. My uncle told me to do what was best for me because nobody can live my life but Kia. He also said that if I wasn't doing anything wrong then I shouldn't let my parents upset me. I followed his advice and did what I thought was best for me.

·

In early 1991 I found out something that has changed my life. I was sitting on my grandmother's bed doing nothing when my mother came in the room and told me that she had something to tell me. My curious ears perked up instantly. She looked at me and said, "What I am about to tell you will upset you." I immediately panicked. She told me that my uncle had been diagnosed as having HIV, the virus that causes AIDS. "He doesn't want you to know," she told me. "So don't say anything until he tells you."

I felt as though my whole world had collapsed. I was really upset and started crying but I agreed to keep quiet. What I did do was try to make it easier for him to tell me. Every time I was around him I would casually mention the topic of AIDS.

One day, about a month after my mother confided in me, my uncle and I were driving in the car and I casually mentioned that I was taking a class that discussed AIDS. I waited a few minutes to see what his reaction would be. He didn't say anything. Then I told him a few of the facts that I had learned. Again I waited. This time he said, "Did your mother tell you I have AIDS?"

I pretended that I hadn't known. But hearing it from him made it seem much more real. I was shocked but I didn't let him know. I decided to drop the subject because all of a sudden I felt uncomfortable talking about it. I had a feeling that from that day on my uncle and I would become even more close. And I was right, we have.

Last year my uncle decided to move to St. Croix for relaxation and peace. When he left it felt as though all the humor had been taken out of our family. There were no more jokes, no more gossip, nobody around to make fun of my father, no one to laugh with, and no more advice. There was also no one to help me release the stress I got from my overprotective parents.

When it finally became too much for me to bear, I got on

a plane to St. Croix. When I got there, I had the time of my life. We rented a jeep and every day we went to the beach. My uncle introduced me to a friend of his who is a lesbian. What a pair they made! I remember sitting on the bed watching videos while the two of them sat there and filled me in on who was a "queen" or a "dyke." In all the years I have been in school, I have never received an education quite like the one I got on that trip.

Luckily for me, my uncle returned from St. Croix a few months ago because the family thought it would be better to have him close to home in case he got sick. He decided to go down to St. Croix every three months instead of living there year-round.

Finding out about my uncle's illness hasn't really changed our relationship. He is still the same person. The only thing that has changed is that I value the time we spend together more. Everything we do I treasure because I have learned that in life there are no guarantees. However, I still treat him the same as I always did. Maybe because I can't or don't want to fully accept what has happened.

The rest of my family has reacted a little bit differently than I have. They've become more possessive and protective of him. These days, my poor uncle is being treated the same way my parents treat me.

My father is the worst. I understand that he is concerned about his younger brother but he tends to go overboard. One day we were in the car going to the bakery and every two minutes he would look at my uncle in the rearview mirror and ask if he was OK. I know this was getting on my uncle's nerves but he acted like it wasn't.

When the two of us go out now, the whole family tells me, "Don't keep your uncle out too long because he will get tired." I want to tell them that he is a grown man with a mind of his own, but I keep it to myself because it is none of my business. My uncle doesn't say anything. I guess he doesn't want to hurt their feelings by telling them to get a life.

Since I found out about my uncle's diagnosis, I have become more aware of HIV and AIDS. People are dying every day, every minute. My uncle told me the best way to ensure my safety is to practice abstinence or safer sex. He told me there is not a man in the world worth dying for. I agree 100 percent.

Sometimes I get sad if I think about my uncle not being here. I do two things when this happens—I pray to God to protect him and then I picture him talking about somebody (usually my father) and that makes me start to laugh to myself. That makes me start to feel like he's not going anywhere.

I even told my uncle that I know he will be sitting in the first row when I graduate from high school *and* from college. I also informed him that he has no choice but to come to my wedding. And, knowing me and how long that will take, I can guarantee my uncle will live for a very long time.

QUILT

Andrew Sullivan

Andrew Sullivan is the editor of *The New Republic*. He lives in Washington, D.C. and Provincetown, Massachusetts.

I first saw the AIDS quilt three years ago, on its last trip to Washington, when it was only a few thousand panels in size and fit comfortably in the Ellipse in front of the White House. Last weekend, at 26,000 panels (one-sixth of the number of deaths in the United States so far), it filled most of the vast space between the Washington Monument and the Reflecting Pool. Neither experience was forgettable; and neither still even faintly morbid. Like the Vietnam Memorial, a few minutes' walk away, the quilt has to be entered in order to be understood; a piece of interactive architecture of both public and private space. But unlike the Vietnam Memorial, the quilt is a buoyantly colorful, even witty, monument. It doesn't immortalize its commemorated in regimented calligraphy; its geography is not that remarkable, black snowdrift of casualties, but a kind of chaotic living room, in which the unkempt detritus of human beings—their jeans, photographs, glasses, sneakers, letters—are strewn on the ground, as if expecting the people to whom they belonged to return. People walk over this cluttered landscape, looking like tourists, caught between grief and curiosity, saying little, peering intently down at the ground. As you approach the quilt from the rest of the Mall, toward a place where tens of thousands of people are congregated, noise actually subsides.

The panels themselves are tacky and vital, and therefore more chilling: you are invited to grieve over faded Streisand albums, college pennants, grubby bathrobes, cheesy Hallmark verses, and an endless battery of silk-screen seventies kitsch. Unlike the formulas of official memorials, each panel manages to speak its own language in its own idiom; you have to stop at each one and rethink. Camus suggested in *La Peste* that the most effective way to conceive of large numbers of deaths was to think in terms of movie theaters, but the quilt dispenses with such mind games by simply reproducing shards of the lives of the fallen, like overheard, private conversations. Some panels are made by lovers, others by parents, friends, even children of the dead; and some are made by those whose names appear on them and speak with uncanny candor. "Life's A Bitch And Then You Die," quips one. Even the names themselves rebel against any attempt to regiment them. In the program, some people are identified with full names, others with first names, others with nicknames. There are sixteen Keiths; and one Uncle Keith; twenty-eight Eds; one Ed & Robert; eighty-two Davids; one David Who Loved the Minnesota Prairie; one mysterious David–Library of Congress; and one David–Happy Birthday. Some go only by two initials–T. J.; others spell it out in full– Dr. Robert P. Smith, Arthur James Stark Jr., HM1 James T. Carter, USN; others are reduced to symbols–five stars (unnamed) "commemorating five theater people who have died"; still others are summoned up by nothing but a baseball cap and an epitaph. Celebrities, of course, creep in–I counted four Sylvesters and twenty-nine Ryan Whites—but they are scattered randomly among their peers. The most piercing: Roy Cohn's. A simple inscription: "Bully. Coward. Victim."

The democracy of the plague is enhanced by the unending recital of names over the loudspeaker, as friends and relatives and strangers read out the death roll. The names resonate with metronomic specificity, adding an aural dimension to the visual litany. "Patrick J. Grace, Dan Hartland, Ron Lopez, Edwina Murphy, Mark Jon Starr, Billy, Kim John Orofino, Frank, Bob Flowers, Sergeant Rick Fenstermaker, U.S. Marine Corps . . ." Many of the two-minute recitations end in "and my brother and best friend" or "my sweet little sister" or some such personal touch. From time to time, a mother's voice cracks over "my precious son and best friend," and the visitors to the quilt visibly stiffen at once, their throats caught in another, numb moment of unexpected empathy. I bumped into an acquaintance. "What's going on?" I asked, lamely. "Oh, just looking for friends."

Just when you're ready to sink into moroseness, however, the panels turn on you. Since this act of remembrance is one our public authorities have not sanctioned (neither President Reagan nor Bush walked the couple of hundred yards to visit the quilt), it is mercifully free of decorum. Drag-queen creations—taffeta, pumps, and pearls embroidered across silk—jostle next to the overalls of manual workers and the teddy bears of show-tune queens. There's plenty of bawdiness, even eroticism, and a particularly humanizing touch you don't find in cemeteries: a lot of the spelling is wrong. Many of the epitaphs have a lightly ironic edge to them, coming close to a kind of death camp: "The Fabulous Scott Tobin"; "Dennis. We Didn't Get To Know Each Other Very Well, And Now We Never Will." My favorite panel ornament was a Lemon Scent Pledge furniture polish can. Others simply shock you into reality: "Hopefully the family now understands" inscribed beneath a pair of someone's jeans; "For the friend who still cannot be named—and for all of us who live in a world where secrets must be kept." And another: "You still owe me two years, but I forgive you and will always love you. I never located your parents. Maybe someone will see this and tell them."

The point of it all, of course, is not merely to release grief, but to affirm the dignity of those who have died so young and in the face of unique public disdain. For many of the families who came to D.C. last weekend, the event was the end of an extraordinary journey to grapple not simply with their loved ones' deaths, but with their lives. A few short years ago virtually everyone I saw at the quilt was gay. This time the presence of families—predominantly heterosexual—was overwhelming. These were ordinary people who through their loved ones' deaths were asserting, beyond their own sorrow, the overcoming of their own shame. Being there was a catharsis not simply of the horrors of the disease, but of the bigotry that stalked so many of those on the ground and, by association, those who reared them. This is one way in which AIDS has surely changed America. With the collapse of the closet, a collapse accelerated by HIV, attacks on gay people are now attacks on our families and friends as well. They will no longer go unanswered. "I have done nothing wrong. I am not worthless. I do mean something," as one panel put it. "This is my beloved son," echoed another, "in whom I am well pleased."

A BEAUTIFUL DAY
IN THE WEEK

Patrick Hoctel

Patrick Hoctel is a writer and editor who lives and works in San Francisco. His fiction has been published in *Christopher Street*, *The James White Review*, and in the anthologies *Men on Men 1*, *Certain Voices*, and *The Gay Nineties: An Anthology of Contemporary Gay Fiction*. He holds an MFA in Creative Writing from the University of Arizona and is currently an assistant editor at the *Bay Area Reporter*.

FOR WILLIAM LOUDEN BATTEN

September 1990

Everyone threatening to quit the paper. No ideas on what to do next. They'll just quit. Will and I have a fight—I think. We're watching Peter Jennings or one of those guys, and there's a commercial for Cher's latest flick. After the TV goes back to the news, I see Will has that "I don't understand at all" look on his face. I pretend not to notice. He asks me the name of the movie, and I tell him, and he seems to get it. But then a minute later, he says, *"Mer* what?" *"Mermaids."* That doesn't do it. *"Mermaid?"* And I tell him that it's plural with an "s" on the end. He's more puzzled, not less. *"Mermen,"* he says. "Why's that?" I sort of exploded and said *Mermaids* about nine times, and then he didn't say anything until after the news. When he gets up to put his dishes in the sink, he says, "You know I have a hearing loss in my right ear." But I think it's the toxo. It's not that he doesn't hear, but things are starting not to register. Al calls at 11:15 P.M.: "I'm definitely going to quit. Maybe I'll stay through Christmas/New Year's, but I've got to get out of there."

November 1990

Ed and I intruded on Mr. and Mrs. Batten's cocktail hour. They've been with us for a week—staying in the front room. Every evening at six it's the same thing: Manhattans. These drinks could knock over a horse, so I revert to my Southern upbringing and sip, sip, sip. Jeanne and Bill are so much like my own mom and dad it's scary. It's the Hoosier connection. They're all from the same part of Indiana—Elkhart, La Porte, Union Mills, etc. Both sets of parents are thrilled that the other grew up around where they grew up, even though they didn't/ don't know each other and my parents live in Louisiana.

Bill: "What Will needs is some fresh air. Some exercise. He's cooped up way too much here." Jeanne said nothing, nada. No mention of the A-word. We nursed our cocktails and worked on not exchanging words or glances. Bill can't give it up. "He used to be such a hiker. Camping, hiking, outdoors." I felt a little pinched at the "cooped up" remark, like Ed and I are Will's keepers or something, even though I know Bill's a little antsy— he's been cooped up in a strange house, in a strange city, with a dying son, with nothing to do.

The phone rings right when I'm about to say something about the neuropathy in Will's feet and legs—so that's good— even though it's our tenant complaining that he can't get his heater to work. Ed goes downstairs. That's when they tell me they're taking Will home for Thanksgiving. "They want to get Will out of the house" is what the voice in my head tells me. But later Will tells me that he wants to go–when they're out having dinner on Potrero Hill. "I'm bringing the family together," he says in his slightly supercilious way. It's cute and true. The four sisters and the parents and he are all talking for the first time in years. But I still think of Bill this morning, pushing the cats away with his foot and saying, "I guess they're how Will got that toxoplasmosis." It gave me bad thoughts. Ours is a toxic house.

November, later that week

Ed and I are rushing out to *Henry and June.* We're late already. No warm coat. Jeanne's standing in the kitchen by the stove next to Will's big blue pot. Jeanne: "I've made vegetable soup. A lot of it. For everyone. Please have some." We explain that we're late, and she understands, but it doesn't help. Her face scrunches up, tears. "I just want to be useful," she says. Bill's on the couch in the living room, but he doesn't hear, doesn't stir. Everything's frozen. Me and Ed putting on our coats, her with the wooden spoon in mid-air. Then I tell her how she's been useful, all the things she's done for Will, arranging his meds in a schedule where he can keep them down, just being here. It's still not enough.

One A.M. House quiet, cold. Ed and I have two heaping bowls of semi-warm vegetable soup. "She'll know if we just throw it out," he says.

December 10, 1990

Seven months at this rag, and still all anyone talks about is quitting. *Mes vacances* is in less than two weeks, and I'm ready. Now the downstairs refers to me as "Sister Death." When an obit comes in, they'll buzz me and say, "Calling Sister Death." That's what I get for working at a gay paper—lowbrow queen humor. The first couple of times it was funny, but these girls don't know when to let up.

A guy came in today on a walker, lesions like his face was a topographical map done in purple, with his lover's obit. It was three and a half pages typed, single-spaced. I told him we weren't supposed to accept anything over 200 words. That was our policy. It was printed on the obituary page. He thrust his lover's resumé at me. He'd been a ceramicist. He'd shown in Germany, in Cologne. In Japan. The guy was almost shaking himself to pieces, so I took the obit and managed to get 850 words in without anyone noticing.

Last week a woman reporter, straight but nice, from the *L.A. Times* called and wanted to know what it was like to be in the midst of this epidemic and handling the death notices for so many men, some of whom I must even know. Good guess, that. So I told her the usual. That I looked upon the free service our paper was providing as an outlet for our community's grief. That the obituaries were a sort of historical documentation of this time in our history. Of future use. That I was concerned, even though it just might be my imagination and not statistically accurate, that the dying seemed to be getting progressively younger. More people in their twenties.

December 25, 1990

Christmas at Mom and Dad's! Ed in New Orleans for first time! We make love in the Vieux Carre at Ursuline Guest House! Film to follow!

After agreeing that it was too much work and we'd go out to dinner, Mom made her traditional Christmas spread: ham basted with Coca-Cola, molded salad with pecans on top, that Lipton onion ring-and-string bean casserole, and for dessert,

McKenzie's pudding cake. Yum, yum. Me: "Is this low-fat?" They didn't get it. Candy all over the house—kitchen, living room, den, bedrooms. I'd forgotten that.

Post-dinner, Ed and Dad went out to the shop. Dad: "I want to show Ed my lathe." While Mom and I adjourned to the den for coffee and tiny cookies. "Cookie bits," she called them. This division was so Ricky-Fred, Lucy-Ethel, if they'd lived in the 'burbs. Maybe I wanted to see the lathe, too. (Okay, I didn't.)

She asked about Ken, she asked about Will, she asked about how I handled Michael's death. Did I write his parents? Even during a plague, etiquette must be maintained. Mom had to ask. Other moms might not have, but Mom is a Southerner, albeit a transplanted one, and not to do so would have been a *faux pas*. A black mark against her on the manners scale. She was saddest about Ken—I think because we spent an evening in his Alamo Square apartment whose living room overlooked downtown SF. Mom: "That was certainly a beautiful view." Real wistful, as if the cruelest thing about this disease might be to have to give up your fabulous apartment and move into a studio in the Tenderloin. But she cares; she's written him cards, encouraging words, in the past.

Then Mom said: "A lot of my friends have died, too." Me: "Yes, Mother, but you're seventy, and I'm thirty-four." Mom: "Well, a lot of your friends died when you still lived here. Before AIDS." That's true. Eddie and Charles O.D.'d. Robert was murdered. Cissy killed herself with her father's shotgun one morning when the family was at Mass. But is this supposed to make me feel *better*?

January 14, 1991

Screaming when I come in the front door. I follow it upstairs through the house to the kitchen. Will is throwing paper and sugar around the room. (Why sugar? It's so hard to clean up. Later Will tells me that the sugar spilled on the forms, but he forgot. He was not throwing the sugar around on purpose.) He yells: "Fucking forms. Same fucking forms I filled out last month for a different thing." I want him to sit down because his balance isn't good. "Fucking insurance morons." It's difficult, painful for him to breathe with the lesions, candida, thrush, etc. in his throat, so I give him some of his smelly (like cat piss) donkey tar tea to shut him up. Will: "They think you'll quit if they keep sending this shit." He starts to choke, and I sort of follow, sort of lead him to the bathroom where he vomits a thin gray spittle into the toilet bowl. He smiles. We both do. Will: "I have to stop triggering my gag reflex." I take the papers—twelve pages—away for a while, and he's right. Not only do they require three different doctors'/care providers' signatures, but they are the same forms he filled out last month, just in different colors. I feel like calling Blue Cross/Blue Shield and scaring somebody bad, so they wouldn't leave the building unless escorted by a guard.

January 26, 1991

Will has had a mad-on for two weeks. Got into a fight with a woman on the Muni because her kid was pulling on his scarf. Will didn't say how old the kid was, but the woman didn't do anything. Just pretended nothing was happening. Will: "Can't you supervise your child?" She screamed at him to mind his own business. Then the other passengers got into it, taking sides. Some for Will, some for her. The kid got interested in a gum wrapper. This morning Will was talking in a very loud voice, not yelling but agitated, to someone on the phone. His door was closed, but I could hear him in the hall. I wanted to make sure *somebody* was on that phone. Will: "I turned off the answering machine because I didn't want any more messages. 'I'm just calling to see how you are. Just checking in.' Can't somebody call now to give me ... blowjobs. Well, I'm sick. That's obvious. Today is better than yesterday, but do you really want to hear about my sputum, my BMs? I don't know what's happening. Nobody does. Only God." Will, a Radical Faerie atheist pagan Druid Celt Dalai Lama lover, has "gotten religion," sort of, as of late. The *Book of Common Prayer* on his desk, the portrait of Jesus from his grandmother's house—when you look at it, after a while the eyes open.

March 10, 1991

I am thirty-five today, officially middle-aged. In 1976 I read somewhere that this is the end of youth. I am halfway through my life span—according to statistics at any rate. However, last week in the *Examiner*, it listed thirty-five as the onset of *early* middle age, followed by middle middle age, and late middle age. Another one of those baby-boomer lifestyle features they're so fond of. What's early old age? When does that begin? Of course, I could also get hit by the proverbial truck—or more likely a bus in this city—crossing the street. At least I have a life span to be halfway through. Will and Angela and his sister Beth are coming from the hospice to get his stuff this afternoon. He's made the decision to go back to Elkhart. The hospice attendant said, "To live." Will said, not missing a beat, "To die."

It was Will and me and Angela and Beth and Ed and Mimi and Lewis and Nancy and Greg and five or six other of his closest friends, his support group. (Scott didn't look so hot.) In all the years Will's lived with me and Ed—five—two months after we moved in together, I'd hardly ever met any of his friends, only the boyfriends. Mimi: "Will kept all of his friends compartmentalized. He was afraid we'd meet and like each other too much. Will has lived in the room next to mine and Ed's since 1986, but I'd never realized just how much stuff he has:

every Eddie Bauer shirt; a half-dozen pair of hiking boots; chaps, vest, cap; boxes of photos, slides, postcards, and letters; small woven baskets full of crystals, shells, bells, volcanic rocks, beads; records, tapes, and CDs; candles; and *beaucoup* journals that stop after a few pages, the rest blank.

We used to make fun of all the catalogs he got at the house, but now I see he really used them. He got peevish, irritated, when we called him a "catalog queen." Beth wanted us all to assemble behind Will for a picture, so the other sisters and the nieces and nephews back in Indiana could see his "California family." Will was clearly—to me anyway—not pleased with the idea but didn't protest. He was always vain about his looks, and with good reason, he was a handsome guy. Long before I met Ed, I tongue-kissed Will at the front door of my house on Haight Street after a Radical Faeries meeting. He was surprised. So was I. It never happened again. One of the hardest things was when the lesions started popping up on his neck, scalp, forehead, and face—areas clothes didn't cover. Today there was a new one—purple and black and angry—on the tip of his nose, giving him a Rudolph sort of look. We got into place, Will sitting on a chair, some strain, but Beth snapped the picture and we all reacted appropriately and automatically, except at the last second Will pulled his beret down. The defiant one.

It hit me when I was trying to find one of his Stephen Levine books up in the loft by his futon that this, of course, was it. His myriad things would still be here, but Will wouldn't. Tomorrow morning he flies out. On the way down the stairs, back to the car, Will was unsteady, hitting the banister with his cane. "Patrick," he said, "I didn't get you a present. What is there of mine you want?" I didn't even have to think. I'm a greedy boy. "That little bell of yours. It's a dinner bell in the shape of a woman. From China." Will whispered so Beth couldn't hear: "I stole that from a friend of my mother's."

March 17, 1991

WILL'S LIST

Richard–*juicer*
Piano–*Radical Faeries in Oregon c/o Oskrr*
Terry and Richard in Ukiah–*2 futons, comforter, and linens. Also,*
    chaps, vests, cap, and boots
Lin and Rene–*pictures, slides, etc. to divide*
Lin and Patrick–*postcard boxes to divide*
Lewis–*tools*
Ed–*drill press and saw*
Scott–*synthesizer and rest of musical instruments*
Angela–*wind harp and CD player*
Family–*package of contact sheets of stone sites*
Plants–*whoever*

Will, as it turned out, had promised the synthesizer to three people. I think he just forgot and wanted everyone to have something nice from him. Scott, his original choice, wound up with it, but it was funny when all three kind of claimed it. In the midst of all the dividing of possessions and lots of tea and coffee and Pepperidge Farm cookies, we called back to Elkhart at a prearranged time, five P.M. there. Will talked to a few people (Scott, Nancy, Lewis, Mimi), and messages were relayed. Will: "I haven't gotten all my Stephen Levine books yet." A remark meant for me but told to Nancy. And, ever the fashion plate, "I want my new hightops sent." By the time it was my turn, he was too tired to talk, so I talked to Beth, his youngest sister–his buddy among the Battens. Beth: "I'm afraid that it'll all fall apart when he goes." I knew what she meant. A crisis gave a family a center, something to focus on and group around. It reminded you of how and why you were a family in the first place, what that was for. Beth: "He's ordering everybody around." And as if on cue, in the background, I heard Will say to his father: "Bring the CDs closer. There. Not there." Definitely a command.

March 26, 1991

Beth called at end of Oscar party last night. Danny and William, Martha, and John had already left. Barbara Walters was interviewing Whoopi Goldberg, who was about to reveal her real name (Caryn Johnson), when the phone rang. Jack: "Let it ring." He was enjoying the show, both of us commiserating over the fact that our fave, Anjelica Huston, had lost out to Kathy Bates in yet another miscarriage of Academy justice. Ordinarily I would have let the machine get it, but I'd been expecting this call.

Ed was in another part of the house with Andy. Funny that it was Jack and Andy who were still here. Will had a huge crush on Andy when they both worked at UCSF, but felt that Jack had put a stop to any extramarital ideas Andy might've had, even though they had an "open relationship."

Beth was teary off and on, but pretty controlled. I'd like to have cried a little but, as usual, couldn't. Will'd died a couple hours before in bed with his teddy. He'd just had a popsicle, which Jeanne had given him. It was a "peaceful" death. I wanted to ask if Will was alone when he died. It sounded like Jeanne had given him the popsicle, then went out, then came back to find him gone. But I didn't have the nerve. Didn't want to sound like I was blaming someone if he died by himself. But I was curious about what that last moment was like.

We talked about Will and how his insurance money was enabling the only sister who didn't have a house to get one. How his death had been a gift to the family, something he shared with them all. I agreed to call a bunch of people. Jack asked who it was, but I shrugged him off, pretended to be listening to Whoopi talk about *Ghost.* I didn't call anyone till this morning. I was hogging his death. I didn't tell Ed or Andy when they came back to the living room. After the news left my lips, it would become the property of the world, the phone lines would gear up, and I had to digest it in some way first.

I told Ed a while after Jack and Andy had gone, and he immediately said: "That was what the phone call was about." He was hurt, I think, that I hadn't told him right away, but I used the excuse that Jack and Andy were here and I wanted to tell him when it was just us two. In truth, I didn't want any kind of input, any common sense "He's out of it now" or "No more pain," etc. I couldn't have stood anyone saying Will's name.

April 29, 1991–day after Will's 37th birthday

Got sick yesterday on the hike at Pt. Reyes. Two hours in, two hours out. No fog, completely clear, and I didn't bring a hat. Wound up with sunstroke–nauseated and out of it. Worst moment was when we were all sitting in a circle on the bluff where Will's ashes were scattered–me and Ed, Jeanne and Bill, Beth and Ned, Mimi, Lewis and Lynne and their daughter, Nancy and Greg, Scott, etc.–and Jeanne turns to me and says, "Patrick, I want you to share with everyone what you wrote Bill and me in your letter. It was so beautiful."

And there I was leaning against Ed with my black sweater over my head, looking like Anna Magnani in *The Rose Tattoo*, and I couldn't recall what she was talking about. And then everyone was staring at me, waiting. I tried to fake it and jabbered something, then mumbled that I really wasn't feeling well, then ducked my head. Jeanne: "Patrick wrote that right before Will went to the hospital for the last time, he said to him that he wasn't afraid anymore–or angry or worried. That he knew that his life was not going to end with his death. That it would continue through all of you and us–his friends and his family."

Actually, I remember thinking that that was a little corny. Corny but nice and, for Will, true. I was glad he'd said it, but we both were slightly embarrassed and didn't look at each other again for a while. That day, the day he told me that, was the day I knew Will was going to die. I'd sort of felt that he'd fooled me and Ed, that he'd made us believe that he was going to be one of the ones to beat it. Right after he'd moved in with us, he'd tested positive, and then there'd been various ups and downs, but he'd been pretty healthy for four and a half years. The last six months were a swift decline. Jerry and I were dressing him that day to go to the hospital. He didn't want to go because he was afraid he wouldn't come back.

I'd tried not to see what AIDS had done to Will's body, his looks, because they were so important to him and he was always disguising the ravages. Maybe it was having someone else in the room with me while Will was naked that made me take stock. His scalp was too tight, flaky, the color a putty gray. The skull had emerged from his face. The lesions had grown and joined together on his chest. They'd gone from minor discolorations, like a forgotten bruise, to these raised, embossed lumps that resembled iridescent algae in the bright overhead light. Greenish tinge around the edges. The hairy little bubble butt that Will had thrust for years into jeans a size too small had now disappeared, a sheer drop from his bony back to his stick legs. Will: "One of my goals is to get my ass back."

Will kept drifting away from us while we were trying to get his shirt on, pants up. I thought he was going to topple off the chair, and then how would we explain that? It would seem so careless. After we'd managed to get him dressed, down the stairs, into my car, and to the hospital to emergency, Jerry said that he thought for a moment while we were dressing Will that Will had died and then come back. I'd felt that, too. Like he had willed himself back to life when he could just as easily have gone the other way.

There was a certain tension in our circle on the bluff. Some of the Sunday hikers were upset that those who'd hiked in the previous day had already scattered Will's ashes before they'd gotten there. I thought it was okay. Maybe it was the sunstroke, but he was here and we were here, so what difference did it make if he was still in a container or not? When it came my turn to talk, I said how I'd never much liked my own brother growing up—we'd never gotten along—but Will had been part of my family with Ed for five years and he was my brother. Like most family, we'd had our differences, but I couldn't imagine living in the house without him, even though I knew it really was final. That was the only reason I'd wanted to see the ashes—to dip my finger in Will and know that he wasn't coming back, from Indiana or anywhere else.

May 25, 1991

I'm seeing Will now. Just in flashes. Out of the corner of my eye. And he's happy, jovial even. No lesions and his weight is up. I haven't shared this with Ed or anyone else. It's questionable. When Tamara lived downstairs, she said the house was haunted, and she and Will would compare notes on the Edwardian spirits/poltergeists they'd encountered. It's so quick I can't be sure, but it makes me sad even though I feel better afterward. "Sad Can Make You Happy" sounds like a Smokey/Marvin Motown standard.

Bit by bit, Ed and I are retaking the room. It's so white except for the loft and all the shelving and the big burn mark in the corner of the loft where Will's candles to Vishnu flamed. My clothes are hanging in his closet, and all the dirty clothes baskets are in here. Mildew smell, but the cats always want to come in. "Undignified" is all I can think. Will had a certain dignity and a lot of pride. Scott at the celebration at Pt. Reyes: "Will and his damn pride." (Our first roomie fight after Will moved in. The plumbing was screwed up, and Will stood at the top of the stairs and announced, "I cannot live in a house where I can't take a hot shower every morning.")

I know Ed wants to do something with the room. Yeah, yeah, yeah, we could use the space. He hasn't pushed yet. At night I'll go down the hall and then jump into the room, hoping to catch a glimpse, a glance, Will unawares. It's stupid, but I have this feeling if I do it spontaneously, in a non-premeditated fashion, just right, it'll work. No, I don't think that, but I do it. More times than I'll ever admit.

DREAMS OF WILL

I've had two. One I don't remember, except for the very end when Will asked me to call Beth. The other I had last night/this morning. My last one before I woke up.

Will appears in the kitchen from the landing around where the cat bowls are. Starts washing breakfast dishes. There's egg on them. (I'm sitting at the table in my robe.) Very friendly, upbeat, smiling, chatty. Like when Robert was murdered in New Orleans so many years ago and came to me in dreams and was constantly reassuring me about how great things were now. Not to worry.

For some reason I'm annoyed. I say, "Will, you know you're dead, don't you?" He exclaims something like, "Of course" and keeps on washing. He doesn't want me to ask more about this, just to have a regular conversation. But I say, "What's it like being dead?" And he says, "Small." The dream starts to break up as I ask him to describe death more, and finally he says as I'm coming out of the ether, "A beautiful day in the week."

A DAY
IN THE LIFE

Denise Ribble

Denise Ribble is the community health educator for the Community Health Project in New York City.

It was the end of a long day. And a long week.

I was sitting at my desk, pondering for the umpteen millionth time how to get a woman enrolled in an Ampligon trial (the testing program for an experimental AIDS treatment), when all the studies to date were stating that being a gay man (or at least pretending to be) was part of the inclusion criteria.

Tacy poked her head in the door and said, "Do you want to talk to someone you don't know who won't give her name?"

"Yeah, sure," I said, glancing at the clock: 6:00 P.M. Why do people always wait until late on Friday to call?

"Hello, this is Denise Ribble, the health educator at the Community Health Project. How can I help you?" I asked.

"You spoke to my friend Mary several days ago," said a soft voice. "She said you would be able to help me. I think I'm at risk for AIDS."

After a few seconds of mental sorting, I recalled Mary as an ex-I.V. user and prostitute who had called on Tuesday.

"Why do you think you're at risk?" I said. There was a pause. "Can you talk there? Is someone listening?" The pause continued. "I'll ask some questions and you can answer, okay?"

"Yes," said the voice.

"Did you ever shoot or skin-pop drugs?"

"No," said the voice.

"Did you ever have sex with bisexual or gay men?"

"I'm a lesbian. I've never had sex with a man," the voice said.

"Did you have a transfusion in the last ten years?" I asked, running through my mental checklist of possibilities.

"No," said the voice.

"So why do you think you're at risk for AIDS?" I wanted to know, running out of patience.

"I'm a vampire," said the voice, ever so softly.

"Oh," I said, like the frog in the wide-mouth-frog joke. It was my turn to pause. A long pause—while I frantically tried to remember what I had learned from Bram Stoker, *Dark Shadows* and *Interview with a Vampire*. (I took into consideration that this was a joke.)

"What exactly are your risky practices?" I asked in my best professional tone.

"Well, when I go to the bars, I make sure I pick up women who are having their periods, and I have oral sex with them."

"Is there any way you can change your practices?" I said.

"I suppose I could drink the blood of animals," said the voice distastefully, and then continued, "If I'm really a vampire, I don't have anything to worry about because I'm immortal. But if I'm just a fucked-up woman who drinks other women's blood, I'm at risk aren't I?"

"Yes," I said.

There was another pause.

"Can vampires donate a tube of blood for HIV testing?" I inquired gently.

"Yes," said the voice. "I already have an appointment. But I wanted to talk with someone about my real risk and what I can do about it."

"Well, for now you can change your risky practices—that'll reduce your risk if you're not infected," I explained. "And you really should wait at least three months from your last exposure before getting tested."

"And if I tested positive, can I come to your clinic?"

"Yes," I said. I had a brief flash of Catholic school fear—you know, fire, crosses (even though I've been a Buddhist for years). Then, mostly I felt sad. For this woman had not thought herself at risk. Now she was. Despite her unique circumstances, she was frightened and isolated.

Not so different from many other women I had talked to.

LUCKY FELLOW
and
THE LIMITLESS HEART

Fenton Johnson

Fenton Johnson is a novelist, short-story writer, essayist, and journalist. He is a frequent contributor to the New York *Times Magazine* and has published two novels, *Crossing the River* and *Scissors, Paper, Rock*. He is the recipient of numerous awards, among them a National Endowment for the Arts Fellowship in Literature and a Wallace Stegner Fellowship from Stanford University. He teaches creative writing at San Francisco State University.

LUCKY FELLOW

A long year and then some since my companion died of AIDS, and it's a Friday, the birthday of Mark, an old friend whose companion of a decade has been dying-as-we-speak for the last two years. Early in the day I call and offer Mark these options: 1) Coming to my place for lunch; 2) Going out for lunch, my treat. He chooses coming to my place, which on this particular day carries some sad and delicious possibility of making love.

So, fine. I'm enthused at the excuse to leave work to spend a Friday afternoon with drop-dead handsome Mark. We never talk of our companions, dying or dead, but we have established that it has been years since Mark has made love, and nearly as long for me. We've carefully avoided talk of the future, content with holding another person's commiserating hand. (The hand-holding has been mostly metaphorical, Mark being caught up in that man thing, and also after two years of living-with-dying very much into guarding his heart.)

So I go out and buy birthday candles and a couple of chocolate cupcakes and a book for a gift, and come home and wrap the book and set the table and stick the candles in the cupcakes and take a shower.

And I'm climbing from the shower and searching for a clean pair of Calvin Kleins when the phone rings and it's Mark, saying that his companion just got the results from his latest test and it's *Pneumocystis* again, and his doctor has exhausted all drugs to treat it and doesn't know what he can do, and Mark wants to spend the afternoon consoling his companion at this latest, grimmest turn of events.

So, fine. I hang up, get dressed (the ragged old Fruit of the Looms will do) and eat my bowl of soup and one of the chocolate cupcakes and resign myself to resuming work, albeit without much enthusiasm.

And as I'm sitting to my work the phone rings again, and it's Mark again, and the doctor has called back to say there's this one experimental drug he has remembered that he hasn't yet tried on Mark's companion and he's sending it over to start treatment right away. And since for the moment Mark's companion is feeling O.K., all things considered, and since it *is* Mark's birthday, maybe he *will* come over for lunch. So he does in fact come over, and I feed him soup and light the candles on the remaining cupcake. He carves it in two and gives me half, and in his gesture I understand what we both want: that short triumph over fate, over time and memory and circumstance that desire may bring at its best.

And on this day it turns out to be very much at its best. The old confusion of love and sex and death carried (safely) to the limit; a modest act of defiance, a declaration of life, thumbing our noses in the face of the beast.

And then I take his hand and he takes it back and pulls on his clothes and goes home to his dying-as-we-speak companion.

The next day, Saturday, I meet for coffee with Fred, a friend whose companion of twelve years died a couple of months ago. As we talk the sun moves around to the west and catches Fred's graying hair. I'm not certain of his HIV status, but the sun catches his graying hair and the parched skin stretched over his temples—the veins glow blue through the translucent flesh and I'm certain he's taking AZT. I've come to think of this premature aging as a side effect of the drug, or maybe of HIV, or maybe both. I look at my friend so sunk in grief and feel first grateful, then guilty, knowing that however tough things are, at least I have a full year of grieving behind me, and that I, a healthy, HIV-negative man, will surely come easier than he to hope—for another love, another life.

Fred tells how when he started losing weight, his sympathetic boss arranged to hire him full time for the minimum number of months required to qualify him for disability payments. (I was right in my guess about his HIV status.) So he's working in this high-powered venture-capital start-up even though he hasn't any energy or desire to work—he goes to work knowing that everyone around him is working fifty-, sixty-hour weeks, but he just goes in and stares out at the traffic and waits for the day when he can quit and go on disability.

Then he talks of taking his companion's ashes to Paris to scatter and begins to weep and I want to hold his hand but don't—all this death and *I'm* still trapped in that man thing. He's maybe forty, a boyish face. He once looked younger than his years but now he looks older. There's no putting an age to him because his is not an aging that has come about from time's passing. As he speaks he is dwelling not in hope but in memory, and it is this, more than the graying hair, that is making him old.

I walk him to his car and give him a big hug and promise to call, wondering where I will find time in my life, room in my heart for another friend confronting his death.

And now it's a week later, and I have for the first time since my companion's death a real date, with a landscape architect whom I'm taking to a play. Tom, my date, is a nice-looking guy with a steady paycheck—every writer's fantasy. When he tells me he's *reading a novel,* I'm impressed and for a long minute bedeviled by stupid, involuntary fantasies of a partner, someone to fill this void in my life.

So it's after the play and he's driving us back to my car and the air is charged with possibility. Never good at leaving well enough alone, I break the silence by asking what he's reading, which turns out to be Stephen King, but that's O.K., I don't hold it against him. "I'm an Anne Rice fan myself," I say. From *The Vampire Lestat* it's an easy non sequitur to complaining about the mess of blackberry briers my landlord calls a yard. "What you need is a landscape architect," Tom says.

"We'll both be old men before I can afford you," I say.

An awkward pause. Tom clears his throat. "There's something you ought to know," he says, but I know it already, I don't need to be told and I don't want to hear it. I cover his free hand with mine. "Next date," I say.

And now I'm homeward bound after a chaste peck on the cheek from Tom and all I can manage is a sad smile, but the next day when I tell this to a straight friend from the suburbs he looks at me as if I'm losing my mind. And maybe I am; or is this just the difference between those inside the epidemic and those looking on? What have I been brought to? "The lucky fellow," Elie Wiesel writes of the terrorist leader in *Dawn.* "At least he can cry. When a man weeps he knows that one day he will stop."

THE LIMITLESS HEART

It is late March—the Saturday of Passover, to be exact—and I am driving an oversize rented car through west Los Angeles. I have never seen this side of the city except in the company of my companion, who died of AIDS-related complications in a Paris hospital in autumn of last year. He was an only child and often asked that I promise to visit his parents after his death. As the youngest son of a large family and a believer in brutal honesty, I refused. I have too much family already, I said. There are limits to how much love one can give.

Now I am here, driving along San Vicente Boulevard, one of the lovelier streets of Santa Monica, California, west from Wilshire to the Pacific. The street is divided by a broad green median lined with coral trees, which the city has seen fit to register as landmarks. They spread airy, elegant crowns against a movie-set heaven, a Maxfield Parrish blue. Each branch bleeds at its end an impossibly scarlet blossom, as if the twigs themselves had pierced the thin-skinned sky.

My friend's parents are too old to get about much. They are survivors of the Holocaust, German Jews who spent the war years hiding in a Dutch village a few miles from Germany itself. Beaten by Nazis before the war, my friend's father hid for four years with broken vertebrae, unable to see a doctor. When he was no longer able to move, his desperate wife descended to the street to find help, and saw falling from the sky the parachutes of their liberators.

After the war they came to California, promised land of this promised land. Like Abraham and Sarah, they had a single son in their advanced years, proof that it is possible, in the face of the worst, to pick up sticks and start again.

At his home in Santa Monica, my friend's father sits in chronic pain, uncomplaining. Unlike his wife, he is reserved; he does not talk about his son with the women of his life—his wife or his surviving sister. No doubt he fears giving way before his grief, and his life has not allowed for much giving way. This much he and I share: as a gay man who grew up in the rural South, I am no stranger to hiding.

His wife always goes to bed early—partly as a way of coping with grief—but tonight he all but asks her to retire. After she leaves he begins talking of his son, and I listen and respond with gratefulness. We are two men in control, who permit ourselves to speak to each other of these matters because we subscribe implicitly, jointly, unconditionally to this code of conduct.

He tells of a day when his son, then eight years old, wanted to go fishing. The quintessential urban Jew, my friend's father nonetheless bought poles and hooks and drove fifty miles to Laguna Beach. There they dropped their lines from a pier to discover the hooks dangled some ten feet above the water. ("Thank God," he says. "Otherwise we might have caught something.") A passer-by scoffed. "What the hell do you think you're trying to catch?" My friend's father shrugged, unperturbed. "Flying fish," he replied.

I respond with my most vivid memory of his son. He was a wiser man than I, and spoke many times across our years together of his great luck, his great good fortune. Denial pure and simple, or so I told myself at first. AZT, DDI, ACT-UP CMV, DHPG, and what I came to think of as the big "A" itself—he endured this acronymed life, while I listened and learned and participated and helped when I could.

Until our third and last trip to Paris, the city of his dreams. On what would be his last night to walk about the city we sat in the courtyard of the Picasso Museum. There at dusk, under a deep sapphire sky, I turned to him and said, "I'm so lucky," and it was as if the time allotted to him to teach this lesson, the time for me to learn it, had been consumed, and there were nothing left but the facts of things to play out.

A long silence after this story—I have ventured beyond what I permit myself, what I am permitted.

I change the subject, asking my friend's father to talk of the war years. He does not allow himself to speak of his beatings or of murdered family and friends. Instead he remembers moments of affection, loyalty, even humor, until he talks of winters spent immobilized with pain and huddled in his wife's arms, their breaths freezing on the quilt as they sang together to pass the time, to stay warm.

Another silence; now he has ventured too far. "I have tried to forget these stories," he says in his halting English.

In the presence of these extremes of love and horror I am reduced to cliché. "It's only by remembering them that we can hope to avoid repeating them."

"They are being repeated all the time," he says. "It is bad sometimes to watch too much television. You see these things and you know we have learned nothing."

Are we so dense that we can learn nothing from all this pain, all this death? Is it impossible to learn from experience? The bitterness of these questions I can taste, as I drive east to spend the night at a relative's apartment.

Just south of the seedier section of Santa Monica Boulevard, I stop at a bar recommended by a friend. I need a drink, and I need the company of men like myself—survivors, for the moment anyway, albeit of a very different struggle.

The bar is filled with Latinos wearing the most extraordinary clothes. Eighty years of B movies have left Hollywood the nation's most remarkable supply of secondhand dresses, most of which, judging from this evening, have made their ways to these guys' closets.

I am standing at the bar, very Anglo, very out of place, very much thinking of leaving, when I am given another lesson:

A tiny, wizened, gray-haired Latina approaches the stage, where under jury-rigged lights (colored cellophane, Scotch tape) a man lip-syncs to Brazilian rock. His spike heels raise him to something above six feet; he wears a floor-length sheath dress, slit up the sides and so taut, so brilliantly silver, so lustrous that it catches and throws back the faces of his audience. The elderly Latina raises a dollar bill. On tottering heels he lowers himself, missing not a word of his song while half-crouching, half-bending so that she may tuck her dollar in his cleavage and kiss his cheek.

"Su abuelita," the bartender says laconically. "His grandmother."

One A.M. in the City of Angels—the streets are clogged with cars. Stuck in traffic, I am haunted by voices and visions: the high thin songs of my companion's parents as they huddle under their frozen quilt, singing into their breath; a small boy and his father sitting on a very long pier, their baitless fishhooks dangling above the vast Pacific; the face of *su abuelita,* uplifted, reverent, mirrored in her grandson's dress.

Somewhere a light changes; the traffic unglues itself. As cars begin moving I am visited by two last ghosts—my companion and myself, sitting in the courtyard of the Hôtel Salé, transfigured by the limitless heart.

ALL THROUGH
THE NIGHT

Carol Muske Dukes

Carol Muske Dukes is a professor of English at the University of Southern California. Her fifth book of poems, *Red Trousseau*, and her second novel, *Saving St. Germ*, were published in 1993. She has published reviews in *The New York Times Book Review* and has received many awards for her poetry, including Guggenheim, National Endowment for the Arts, and Ingram Merrill fellowships.

Throughout the summer of 1985, my two-year-old daughter was sick. High fevers left her soaked in sweat and her fine hair streaked on her skull, the damp imprint of her hot head on my nightgown. I spooned Tylenol into her mouth, held cool compresses to her brow, bathed her in tepid water: nothing helped.

Every night I rocked her, sang to her, then stared idly at dawn flaring up in the window. Down Sunset Boulevard, a half mile up into the Hollywood hills on King's Road–my friend Paul Monette was also sitting up late, wringing out cloths, frowning at the red suspense of the thermometer against light. He too was tending the sick–his lover of many years, Roger Horwitz.

Despite the similarities, there was a big difference in our late vigils: Annie had a persistent summer cold, from which she would eventually, unquestionably recover. Roger was not going to recover. He was going to die of AIDS.

Paul stared at the thermometer's red horizon and beyond: into a tunnel that narrowed and descended into darkness. Roger would die, there was no hope for him, all of Paul's patient, tender nursing—all those sleepless nights—would cure nothing.

Thinking about that single incontrovertible fact that separated us those wakeful dawns, I recoil: how could I have *compared* our two situations? How can I compare them now? My child was suffering through a slightly unpredictable childhood illness. Even the scary, unstoppable fevers were a sign that her immune system was working and fighting back, according to her pediatrician. Yet Paul and I began to write poems to each other, I realize now, like two mothers sharing a long night in a hospital ward.

There are few written testimonies by mothers about the loneliness of the sickbed vigil. Not much is documented, I think, for obvious reasons having to do with time and a sense of privacy, or whatever that reticence can be called. There is silence on this subject as well because these are the moments when mothers veer closest to despair—and isn't despair the opposite of the maternal? Apart from Mrs. Ramsay in *To the Lighthouse* (caught in the great light's mindless, regularly timed beam), it is a conspiracy of silence and superstition: *let this pass and I will continue to believe.*

But anyone who is awake, watching, in those cold blue-hours, knows what life is worth, knows maternal despair, is a *mother.* Is there any gender or familial role that separates one watching, unsleeping consciousness and another? And the objects of this anxious regard: the sick child, the dreaming lover, the failing friend, the dying brother, sister, parent—there are no differences among the loved, the lost. Each is uniquely the same: indispensable.

During those long nights I could feel my soul growing enormous, an overseeing mind—then small as my sick child's body. I was a mass of alternating energy, gauging the night's intent. Because of those long nights, the spirit of the aubade has changed forever for me. Dawn for me now is Philip Larkin's dawn, the dawn of his famous "Aubade"—no longer a song of waking lovers, rather it is the first light after loss.

Paul and I were united in our confrontation of the illusion of the popular "miracle." We could change nothing, we could heal nothing. A lover's decline into death, a child's succumbing to a lifelong pattern of malady—or a sudden turn from an innocuous cold to the unthinkable.

Lines I later deleted from a poem called "Summer Cold":

> *I haven't said how outside on the lawn*
> *something's at Night's throat, good neighbor Dawn?*
> *That sound of choking, Paul, when I hear that*
> *I believe in nothing, it all goes black.*

How did we start writing to each other? We'd known each other's work on the East Coast (we'd rubbed line breaks in an anthology), and then after we'd moved west, met at a party at Marjorie Perloff's house. I liked Paul and Roger immediately and we became friends.

Not long after Roger had been diagnosed, Paul and I met for coffee. I didn't know yet that Roger had AIDS, Paul had decided not to talk about it in the beginning—but I remember, as we talked, a *shadow* over us. I'm not sure that Paul ever did tell me about Roger in so many words: I sensed it from his expression, his hesitancy when I asked after Roger.

That afternoon over cappuccino, we hinted at our anxieties in broader terms. I missed New York, though I loved my baby.

I was a little lonely, my actor husband was away sometimes for months at a time. Paul missed writing poems, he'd been blocked for a while. We stared sadly at each other. One of us, I think it was me, suggested that we write poems to each other, a verse correspondence: we called it a "conspiracy," as in "breathing together." We shook on it, we toasted each other: the afternoon sun poured through a skylight above, the shadow passed by.

I had no hint of what would happen. What I saw, in the beginning, as a postal tête à tête, a gentle badinage, turned—on Paul's side—into a flood, a cataract of undammed emotion. Words he couldn't locate, face to face with me over coffeecup, came pouring through my mail slot.

He wrote most of the poems that became *For Love Alone, Eighteen Elegies for Rog*—all the fury and despair and terror found voice. By contrast, my stuttering, small and less-frequent poems found their way to him and he *answered* them. He listened to me writing about a sick baby, a recurring dream about an old New York apartment, breast-feeding.

Now I realize (ashamed!) re-reading the correspondence, how strongly Paul, despite his fear and his anger, was able to express his concern for me, to identify with *my* terrors. And how little comfort I provided for him.

At first he seemed a little resistant to the mother theme:

> *No I am not Mrs. Ramsay*
> > *nor was asked.*
> *Was further given to understand*
> *this room would overlook the Spanish Steps.*
>
> . . .
>
> *Can we just do this: tennis it*
> *back and forth*
> > *talk the dark to death . . .*
> > > *(Severn, quick—*
> *draw him now! He's breathing!*
> > > > ("PM to CM, 7/16/85")

Ah God, but Severn was a mom, was he not? When I answered with my poem "Summer Cold," Paul sent me a devastating poem about Roger.

Then I sent him "Dream" about an old apartment of mine in New York City, which he answered immediately in his best Ronald Firbank persona:

> *Ah yes, the house dream. You've come*
> *to the right place: the only poet*
> *in Cambridge Mass with a life*
> *subscription to* House and Garden
> *rather than* Parnassus.

We were off. He sent me "Ici Tombe" referring to the "white stripe snake" in Franklin Canyon, fed "one medium mouse a month" and signed it "PM to CM, 7/20, Hail, co-conspirator!"

I lobbed a slow poem back, which began: "When you wrote me/about the mouse they feed to the white-stripe snake in Franklin Canyon," ending up: "how I never learned the right way questions are to be asked."

I wrote to him about allergies and the immunological protection breast-feeding is supposed to provide the nursing infant—trying to link this process with AIDS. And failing, I might add. It ended:

> *…a bird is singing, the long white jets translucent*
> *out of the nipple—*
> not the self, but what the self can contain.

Suddenly, grave frightening love poems and angry poems began to flow from Paul. A poem he later published called "The Worrying" caught the mood:

> *around the house with a rag of ammonia*
> *wiping wiping crazed as a housewife on* Let's

Make a Deal *the deal being PLEASE DON'T MAKE*
HIM SICK AGAIN . . .

As he wrote the poems, his prayers were not being
answered. Roger got sick again. And again. On October 17, he
writes in a poem's margin:

> CM:
> It's all become such a swirling nightmare lately— thank god for
> this project of ours. This one has taken an unconscionable
> time to write & please forgive me, don't let me break the flow.
> I *need* it, & I love our growing little pile. So much to tell you
> but have no words. Onwards, somehow.
>
> > PM
>
> (Oh did I ever turn 40 this week.)

I'd gone to Paul's fortieth birthday party (marred by Roger's
being too sick to attend) and I wrote a poem for the occasion.
I remember Paul in his tux, smiling, surrounded by people in
glittering evening dress—at the beautiful home of Roger's brother, who later died of AIDS as well. I wrote a poem, "For Paul
on his Fortieth Birthday" using the threatening images that
haunted me.

Roger was being besieged now by "opportunistic" infections. Paul's poems stopped directly "answering" mine and jack-
hammered his obsession home. Friends and friends' lovers were
dying all around him day by day. Paul commingled horror with
irony:

> *Bruce went before I could finish even this*
> *but nobody left him alone nobody changed*
> *we all stayed the giant seldom stars blew off*
> *the night there was no virus in our hearts.*
> ("THE TWICE BORN")

Beneath the poem:

CM:

This isn't fair. This isn't the deal we made. And three months of being crazy at 2 A.M. has not made this poem noticeably shorter, however baroque its enjambment. But I wrote it mostly to keep from going over the edge, & 2 people died in the middle of it, so perhaps it is more of a fever chart than a poem. I don't think I've even given you anything to play off. But maybe we can go back to tennising back and forth, if only this medieval torture chamber will let up a bit. All I know is that these 8 poems are the only record I have of the last year. . . .

PM, 1/16/86

I was the first to send one of our hermetically sealed "private correspondence" poems out to be published. I don't know why. I didn't ask Paul what he thought about "breaking open" our poems. And worse, I deleted the lines of direct address to Paul at the end of my poem "Summer Cold" and sent it to *The New Yorker*. Howard Moss took it. The deletions made the poem surer of itself but less personal. Paul's first knowledge that I'd "gone public" was seeing the poem in the magazine. I've always regretted that I didn't talk to him about it, that I took out the lines to him without telling him.

On the other hand, I'd been working on a long poem called "Applause," which grew out of the PM/CM correspondence. It was a series of sonnetlike meditations on photographs of Paul and Roger, taken by Holly Wright for an exhibit she mounted at Laguna Beach Gallery entitled "Applause"—wonderful portraits of people clapping. I didn't sent it to Paul as I worked on it over the course of our correspondence. It was, I suppose, the statement I couldn't make, week to week, unlike Paul. Meanwhile, Roger worsened, Paul wrote a bitter furious poem about William Buckley recommending the quarantine of AIDS patients. Then his old humor surfaced . . .

> Hoping you will forgive all this bile on Palm Sunday (if only it were a holiday celebrating Wallace Stevens) and thanking you for the mercy lunch and for always making me laugh a bit about the apocalypse. I feel like Pee Wee Herman starring in *King Lear* & if the dishwasher breaks one more time I will literally run amok.
>
> XXX
> Paul

Then, in April, Roger's sight began to fail.

2 A.M., 4/28. Tuesday

> CM – What a joy to come home today and find *Applause*. I didn't even know I was in the show, though I suspected Roger would be, on account of his beaming. The last 3 days have been the longest and cruelest, after Roger woke up with his sight dimming and then gone in two hours, the retina having detached from his one good eye. 3 days of tears & terrors & he was in surgery for 4 hours today, given a 50-50 chance that they could reattach it. And they *did*, so from 4:00 till late tonight I have felt touched by this one small miracle after a torrent of chaos. . .

Months later, after Roger's death, Paul sent me a poem called "The Losing Side," which described his friendship with the mother of a two-year-old who had died and was buried near Roger on a hill in Forest Lawn Cemetery.

> *Eve is five graves over—or Brian is at least—*
> *d. 18 June two years old Eve elbow-rubs*
> *the bronze plaque changes her flowers before*
> *the least brown edge and sticks a pinwheel in*
> *the ground above think what a brave toy it is*
> *to flutter here on the hill . . .*

And again, the margin held the thoughts that made me see and understand what he'd grasped more powerfully than me:

CM–
I wrote this in response to "Applause," I think, because I realized there were things you could write about *my* fears that I couldn't, and maybe the same went for me and yours. In any case it's the first occasion–the first desire?–I ever had to write about a mother, for though she is very sad Eve is a wonderful lady. I had to make it good for her, good for Brian, & so much of what I know about mothering feels like comes from your poems. The fever poem, way back, was full of what *I* felt taking Rog's temp hour by hour, and I always wanted to make that equation in a poem.

(3/2)

Too late, I sit, holding these poems, wondering at Paul, disappointed in myself, seeing so clearly what I couldn't quite see then. It is 1993. My daughter Annie is ten years old and healthy, Roger is dead and buried, Paul is failing now–as I write this in October–dying of AIDS. I want to write him a final poem, telling him what a gift our correspondence was to me too, how I couldn't seem to say it then–but there may not be time for that last envoi. So I've taken this from a journal, Paul, and I send it off with all my love: Hail, o co-conspirator!

That summer day the two of you came over to
my house. Roger: a hug in the doorway, then climbing
the stairs to Annie's room. It was sunny, mid-afternoon,
she was sleeping. He moved to her crib, lay his hand
on her forehead in a kind of blessing. Sleep well, honey,
he said.

I can still see him: his gentle,
intelligent face, his slightly stooped frame, his quick
quick smile. And Paul–you, behind him, a dark

ironic glance taking everything in with a sidelong grin. You said something that got us laughing. We hushed each other. The curtains in the baby's room moved slightly: a breeze, then the brightness dimmed a little: shadow over the sun. We nodded to each other, we went downstairs. A quick shadow, then it was gone.

LETTERS
TO THE DEAD

Marlon Riggs

Marlon T. Riggs was a documentary filmmaker and faculty member at the University of California–Berkeley Graduate School of Journalism. He was best known as director of the Emmy award-winning *Ethnic Notions* and the Peabody award-winning *Color Adjustment,* both of which examine the representation of African Americans in popular culture, and for the much acclaimed *Tongues Untied* on black gay male identity. He died of AIDS in April 1994, at the age of 37.

Dear Gene:

For what seemed the thousandth time I watched *Tongues Untied* a few days ago, this time of all places in Clemson, South Carolina. In a room filled with whites, in a small college town much like that room, I watched the screen and your image flicker by. How strange it was, in so alien an environment, to see you there, larger than life, singing, living, still. I listened closely to the music of your voice—how much you remind me of voices centuries past—your raw-edged tenor blending rhythms and inflections descended from slaves into a hymn, a doo-wop declaration of freedom.

I listened and remembered: on the night of the San Francisco premiere less than two years ago, you rested in a public hospital bed, laid low by pneumocystis. Remember? I dedicated the premiere to you and your quick recovery. And when I saw you days later, your pride and glee were immediately self-evident. So clearly you spoke, so confident you seemed. Alone, you rose from the bed, and went to the bathroom. I watched and I thought, I too have been here, though for different reasons, and I know what effort—what will—so simple a task of rising to urinate requires.

I left you that day, both of us radiantly optimistic about your imminent return home. Two weeks later I was shocked by the news that you had been returned to intensive care. Relapse. At your bedside, I watched you struggle for each, single, irregular breath—each breath a battle between your will and the respirator. A friend lightly clasped your bloated hand. Your eyes flickered, your lips barely moved, I watched your face. Friends bent close to hear you, to decipher your mumbled whisper. But no one understood, and so, as tactile communication, they continued to hold your hand. I watched your face. "You're hurting him," I said. "Holding his hand hurts." The friend released his grasp, and your face, ashy, drawn, immediately relaxed. Within your face I saw my own. Odd. I was not afraid. I studied you as I might study a mirror, witnessed the reflection of my own probable future, my not too dissimilar past. How close I, too, had come to being killed, not by the pneumonia, but by the virus's most lethal accomplice: silence.

"Do you think I'm going to make it?" you asked us, eyes closed, barely a whisper. We looked at one another. No one spoke. Then the man who had once been your lover and had struggled to remain your friend answered: "They're trying a new drug. But you have to rest. You have to stop fighting the respirator. Let it breathe for you. Rest so the drug can start to work."

The drug didn't work. Nor the respirator. You died the next

day. And in my mind's eye I continually watch your face, study the slow drain of life from your dark-brown skin, your eyes, your chapped lips. I often see you as some superimposed photograph, you as you lay dying in the hospital that day, and you upon the screen, standing upright, tuxedoed, finger-snapping, smoothly defiant in your harmonizing doo-wop that we come out tonight.

Tell me, Gene, how is it that you could come through so much—through alcoholism, financial dependency, racial self-hatred, internalized homophobia, neglected hypertension. Tell me how you managed to master each of these demons, yet would not—could not—contend with that most insidious foe: the silence that shields us from the reality that we are at risk, that our bodies might be sites of impending catastrophe. Did you believe, as so many of us still do, that black people "don't get it"?

Dear Chris:

Didn't you say that the black community would pay dearly for denial? I heard you, but did I listen? We were sitting, the two of us, alone in your home, talking more honestly than we ever have. Sex, love, death, disease, denial: our final conversation, remember? "Black gay men," you said, "have fooled themselves into believing they are immune. The black community will pay a price." Coming from a white boy, I thought your words a little harsh. But you explained that AIDS can have a liberating effect on the tongue, lets you lash it like a whip, and get away with it. And I thought to myself: hmmmm, let's store that thought—just in case.

But that "just in case," I now know, was—as far as I was concerned—remote, theoretical. I heard you, Chris, but your message, I felt confident, was not meant for me. And the degree to which I embraced it was out of ideological and political, not personal, necessity.

Oh, don't read me, girlfriend. You know I'm not the only one, though I should have known better. I should have had some sense knocked into me by the sight of my gym buddy, Alfredo. Yes, I should have known better when I saw the peculiar rash on Alfredo's brown, muscled back, a light-colored rash which spread to his chest, his arms, his face. Should have realized something was up when his weight went suddenly down. I watched him drop as many pounds as he once pressed. I watched, while like some sick solitary elephant he wandered off from the herd to die. Alfredo quietly disappeared from the clubs, the gym, disappeared into shadows and the silence of his apartment. When did you die, girlfriend? Even now, I don't think anybody knows, you did it so—discreetly. Yes, Chris, I hear you: and we are paying a devastating price for such "discretion."

Dear Lewayne:

Funny. How crisis has a way of either deepening or disrupting our delusions. Were you watching when the German doctors told me that both of my kidneys had ceased to function, and that I was HIV-positive, to boot? Stunned, silent, yet alert, I lay in that German hospital bed, my inner eyes, at last, beginning to open. Did you see what I saw, Lewayne—Lewayne, spitting image of myself; Lewayne, whose mother/father/family declined to visit you during worsening illness; Lewayne, the first black man I personally knew to join this long, solemn procession: did you see, Lewayne, how quickly, quietly, my delusions of immunity disintegrated? Were you watching, girlfriend? Did you nod and sigh:

"It's about time!"

Sweet Lewayne, who first lost sight, then life, to the raging virus, were you nonetheless my witness? Did you see over the ensuing months of my recuperation what happened to my kidneys, my sight, my tongue? Did you see how slowly, gradually, my kidneys once started to work, how slowly, gradually I began to see the consequences of silence, and how as a consequence of this insight, my tongue unhinged from the roof of my mouth, dislodged from the back of my throat, slipped–free? And in the hospital, like some exuberant runaway escaped from slavery, I sang aloud, with all my might:

> *Oh Freedom*
> *Oh Freedom*
> *Oh Freedom over me*
> *And before I'll be a slave*
> *I'll be buried in my grave*
> *And go home, yes I'll go home*
> *And be free*

Surely, I thought, some nurse would have rushed to the door and hushed me or some less polite fellow patient simply demanded that I shut up all that noise. But no one came and no one protested, so from my hospital bed I continued to sing, with all my might:

> *I shall not*
> *I shall not be removed*
> *I shall not*
> *I shall not be removed*
> *Just like a tree*
> *That's standing by the water*
> *Oh I shall not be removed*

Dear Harriet:

Did you hear, Harriet, the trembling trepidation in my voice (trembling which even now in remembering threatens to repossess me)? And didn't you, like the good shepherd that you have always been, didn't you come–and take my hand?

Beneath the continuous blare of Geraldo, Joan, Oprah, Phil, *The Young and the Restless*, and *All My* oh-so-tedious *Children*, I heard you, Harriet, paid strict attention to your silent command: stand up and walk! Remember, Harriet? Remember while my lover, mother, grandmother, friends, walked me through the hospital hallways with I.V. in tow, you walked with me also, lightly holding my hand. And when we had escaped out of the woods, you pressed me on till we reached the river and you said simply, silently, with your eyes: wade in the water, child, if you want to get to the other side.

How many runaways had you so commanded? How many hung back and clung in fear to what they felt they knew, sought refuge in the woods, thick silence, darkest night? How many thought they could escape by becoming invisible? But didn't you know, Harriet, that slavery is never escaped as long as the master controls your mind? And don't you now see the chilling parallels between the means by which we were held captive in your time, and the methods of our enslavement today? Don't you see the chains, my Harriet, sweet Moses, the chains not so much of steel and the law, but more insidious: the invisible chains, linked over centuries, of silence and shame? In this latest crisis, our new master is the virus; his overseer—silence; and his whip—shame.

Were you watching when I stepped into the deep? I who have never learned to swim was certain I would drown. Chilly, troubled waters swept over my feet, rose gushingly to my ankles, my hips, waist, chest, then my neck. Troubled, angry waters whipped and tore at me, brutally washed away decades of deep-layered shame, washed away the denial, the fear, the stigma; cracked and splintered the master's lock and chain.

Before I knew it I was naked and trembling—and free. And that's when I began to sing, from the hospital bed, and I know I sang off-key, but the quality of the song didn't matter as much as the affirming act of singing:

I woke up this morning with my mind
Staying on Freedom
I woke up this morning with my mind
Staying on Freedom
I woke up this morning with my mind
Staying on Freedom
Hallelu–hallelu–hallelujah

Dear comrades, lovers, girlfriends, family:

Bless you for the blessings you've given me. I know but one way to redeem the precious gift of your lives, your deaths, and that is through living testaments, old and new, to all we have been and might become. For I know that through such testaments we are forever fortified: through such testaments we will keep on walking and keep on talking until we get to the other side.

Marlon

SKILLS AND PILLS

Kate Scannell

Kate Scannell was the head of the AIDS ward at the Fairmont Hospital, San Francisco, when this piece was written. She continues to practice medicine in the Bay Area. "Skills and Pills" has been included in AIDS health workers' training at clinics and hospitals throughout North America.

When I originally set foot in this Bay Area county hospital, I had no intention to work primarily with AIDS patients. Fresh out of university-based medical practice as an internal medicine resident, rheumatology fellow, and bench researcher, I had decided to forgo academic medicine and practice community-based general medicine in my favorite setting, a county hospital. By now, I have been working for more than two years in this county hospital's AIDS ward.

Shortly after my arrival in the hospital, I discovered that a number of beds were taken by AIDS patients. Most of them were about my age, and many were dying. Several of them had arrived in the county health care system through tragic personal circumstances attending their AIDS diagnosis, which had cost them their jobs and sometimes their health insurance. I was overwhelmed by their illness, their very complex medical problems, their awesome psychological and emotional needs, and their dying. I was frightened by the desperation of many who wanted to be made well again or to survive that which could not be survived.

I felt all I really had to offer these patients were the tools in my doctor's bag and this head stuffed with information. So it became imperative that this small offering from me be the best and biggest it could.

During the first few months of my work, I began my hospital rounds with the non-AIDS patients because so much time was involved in the AIDS ward routine. I stayed late hours without meals nearly every day so I could figure out the fever sources, treat the pneumonias, push the chemotherapy, perform the lumbar punctures, and counsel the lovers and families. Like a very weary but ever-ready gunfighter, I stalked the hallways ready for surprise developments and acute medical problems to present themselves; I would shoot them down with my skills and pills. The diseases that would not respond favorably to my treatments and the patients who would die were all my failures, fought to the end. No patient who wanted treatment died because they did not receive aggressive full-service care from me. I became such a sharpshooter for AIDS-related medical problems that the patients with AIDS were soon gravitating to my medical service.

Some patients were so emaciated by profound wasting that I could not shake disquieting memories of photographs I had seen as a little girl which depicted Auschwitz and Buchenwald prisoners. There were young men on the ward who were grossly disfigured by masses of purple skin tumors. One of these men, who had one eye bulging forward and the other closed tight because of his tumors, caused me to have a recurring nightmare about the Hunchback of Notre Dame.

There were so many sad stories and unhappy events on the

ward. I barely spoke of these to my closest friends, and I avoided telling them how I was being personally affected by all the
tragedy and death. I was hesitant to be so serious with my
friends, and I really didn't even know how to verbalize what it
was I was seeing, hearing, and experiencing in the first place.

Months elapsed in this way. One day Raphael, a twenty-
two-year-old man, was admitted to the ward. He was a large,
bloated, purple, knobby mass with eyes so swollen shut that he
could not see. His dense, purple tumors had insinuated themselves into multiple lymph nodes and into the roof of his
mouth. One imposing tender tumor mass extended from the
bottom of his right foot so that he could not walk. His breathing was made difficult by the massive amount of fluid surrounding and compressing his lungs. Tears literally squeezed
out from the cracks between his eyelids. He asked me to help
him. I heard the voices of my old teachers who prodded me
through my years of medical training—I heard them telling me
to fix this man's breathing disfunction, instructing me how to
decipher and treat his anemia, reviewing with me how to relieve
his body swelling with medications while correcting his elec-
trolyte disturbances. I heard these voices reviewing with me the
latest therapies for Kaposi's sarcoma. Raphael asked me to help
him. I stuck needles into his veins and arteries to get more
information about him. I stuck an intravenous line into one of
the few spots on his arm that wasn't thickened by firm swelling
or hard purple tumors.

He asked for more help. I stuck a plastic cannula into his
nose to give him more oxygen. I gave him potassium in his I.V.
line. I told him his problems were being corrected and we could
discuss chemotherapy options in the morning. After I left the
hospital that night, feeling exhausted but confident I'd given
"my all," another physician on duty was called to see my
patient. Raphael asked the physician to help him. The physician stopped the intravenous fluid and potassium, cancelled

the blood testing and the transfusion, and simply gave Raphael some morphine. I was told Raphael smiled and thanked the doctor for helping him, and then expired later that evening.

I think of Raphael often now and I ask him for his forgiveness during my frequent meditations. I also tell him that I have never practiced medicine the same way since his death; that my eyes focus differently now, and that my ears hear more clearly the speaker behind the words. Like the vision of Raphael's spirit rising free from his disease-racked corpse in death, the clothing fashioned for me by years of traditional Western medical training fell off me like tattered rags. I began to hear my own voices and compassionate sensibilities once again, louder and clearer than the chorus of voices of my old mentors. Nowadays, as in an archaeological expedition, I sometimes try to uncover how I had become so lost in the first place. I envision that I got crushed under mounds of rubble that collected over the years of my intense and all-consuming medical training, during which I strove so hard, twenty-four hours a day, to become a physician in the mode of traditional Western medicine. Some of the rubble I can identify as parts of this structure: the trend towards increasing technological interventions; the overriding philosophy that competent physicians save lives, not "lose" them; the blatant chastisement of physicians who use the "sensors" and intuitive insights when interacting with patients; the taboo against using compassion as a diagnostic and therapeutic medical skill.

Shortly after Raphael's death, I assumed the position of clinical director of AIDS services at this county hospital. Subsequently, the targets for my diagnostic sharpshooting abilities became fewer and smaller. I am no longer frightened by this awesome disease and I no longer have nightmares. I cry often and stand the bedside deathwatch frequently. I have been able to communicate with patients now, when I know that I am hearing and seeing them with tremendous clarity, and when I am able to speak clearly to them with the truths I know in my heart as well as my mind. I have substituted ice cream or local bakery products as primary or sole therapy for some AIDS patients with "complex medical disease." I have officially pre-scribed sunshine, a trip to Macy's and massages for some patients who had no need for my traditional skills and pills.

On daily rounds, I have visited a demented AIDS patient whose intermittent cerebral flailings sometimes made him think he was back on his Texas ranch tending the pigs and chick-ens. For days we had discussed the problems a few of the pigs were posing and the most lucrative way to sell eggs; once we made plans to invite the neighbors (other patients on the ward) over for a farm-style breakfast. He never saw my stethoscope or a needle in his arms; I believe he was peaceful and pain-free when he died. As each AIDS patient experiences stages of understanding and accepting of his own disease and death in the Kübler-Ross scheme, I feel I have passed through similar stages as a physician in response to the entire specter of AIDS.

I am currently waddling between grief and acceptance of this disease. I am learning how to temper hope with reality. Through a long period of unhappiness responding to all the death I was seeing, I have been able to find some peace, walk-ing comfortably, day to day, alongside the promise of my own death. And I am grateful to hear my own voices and feel the strength of my compassionate sensibilities once again. I think of Raphael often.

NOW
IS THE TIME FOR
ALL GOOD

James Lecesne

James Lecesne has been creating one-person theater works since 1980, including *One Man Band, Word of Mouth,* and *Everybody's Dream According to Edgar.* He has been a contributor to magazines such as *Details* and *Gourmet,* and his new book, *My First Car,* was published in 1994. Mr. Lecesne also works with Friends in Deed, a drop-in center serving those affected by life-threatening illness. In addition to leading ongoing support groups for those who are HIV-positive, he facilitates a monthly workshop called Healing and Performance, which focuses on the healing properties of self-expression.

July 1993

They want to know about your future. How big it is. If you have one. It's become a matter of status.

"Are you . . . ? I hope you don't mind my asking. I mean, you don't have to tell me, but have you been tested?"

Of course, they're referring to your blood. Has it been tested? But the question always comes out as: Have you been tested?

They don't particularly want to hear about the details. They're not asking about the personal test you went through, the waiting. They're not interested in how you assessed every remembered exchange of fluids since, maybe, 1980, how you counted the lovers, how you forced yourself to name names and review the current "status" of every former and ex- .

No. None of that.

What they want to know is—are you one of us?

There are, it seems, only two possible responses:

Positive or Negative.

Here's where it gets tricky. If you mean to say something positive, something that the World perceives as good (i.e., the illusion of a lot of time), then you must say, "Negative." "I am Negative." If, on the other hand, you mean something that the World regards as not so good, something negative, (i.e., the possibility of limited time), then you must say, "Positive." "I am Positive."

And yes, you will be asked.

But no matter what title you give yourself, whatever the results of your blood test, try to remember that it makes no difference, because regardless of our politics or our preferences, we are all in this together. We all get tipped a little out of our eternal selves every time we begin to think in terms of opposites. Positive or Negative, we all fall headlong into a contracted world of time and measure when we answer.

Look into their eyes when they ask; they are your future.

Once a week, she cooks lunch for the folks here. Simple WASP meals with tantalizing titles: "Perky Cucumber Salad," "Summer Vegetable Soup," "Grandma Allen's Strawberry Square Cake." Delicious stuff. Where once she designed meals for uptown dinner parties and PTA functions, now she plots healthy menus for downtown lunches and functioning PWAs. I admire her, but she assures me that in her book, what she does is nothing more than normal. I like her book and long to live in it.

Over the weekend, a man from here whom she hardly knows calls her and asks a favor—groceries. She complies and walks the hell-hot streets, the six flights up, the whole deal. Afterwards, she sits with him in the cool of his apartment. This, she says, is as close to grace as she has ever known. How wonderful that one must first be asked, she says, to experience this bliss. Service requires two equal partners—one asking, one responding; it works that way. Like everything else that's sacred in this world—circular. Thomas Merton perfectly described the same circle of grace that can occur between God and man—something about how God responds to our call, but only after he calls us in the first place. Our prayers have been answered even before our lips can speak the words.

D.'s spleen is back to its normal size, and though his weight is very low, he is gaining. He looks in the mirror, sees himself, and chuckles: "Who says I'd never live to be an old man? I look just like my grandfather." But that was in the hospital, and the hospital, for the moment, is behind him. He is home now with Bill, the dog, and he takes his six flights, the 140 stairs, in one steady climb without stopping. His food is delivered every day by God's Love We Deliver, and he has more money than he's ever had in his life ("They keep sending checks!") So why, he wants to know, doesn't he feel more grateful? Why doesn't he feel more of everything? And in saying this he is relieved, restored to himself, and he to us. He is living again, and like all of us, he finds himself wanting.

I walk him home. On the street corner we stop to wait for the light to change. Above us the sky is an extravagant gesture of pale blue and peach, and by some trick of light and color, it appears to extend much higher than usual. The neon along Prince Street glows with possibility, and all the sweetness of summers we have known becomes suddenly apparent to us both. He takes my hand and holds it in his.

"I just want to stay here," he tells me. And he cries.

For a moment, I think he means to stay on that street corner forever. But then, as the light changes and we begin to move along, I realize that he meant "here" in the largest sense of the word. I look behind me at that corner; it will never be the same to me. It has eternity in it now.

REALIZATIONS AT BEDSIDE

Mary Jane Nealon

Mary Jane Nealon is a research nurse and poet living in New York City. Her poetry has appeared in *Mid-American Review, Hanging Loose,* and *The Minnesota Review.*

Eighteen years ago I sat in nursing school, my waist-length hair in a tight braid, shoes polished, and listened to our instructors talk about their young careers, with polio and the TB epidemic. Their language was exotic: iron lung, consumption, sanatorium. I had visions of pale poets in huge wheelchairs on the grass, magnificent trees above them, fresh air.

These nurses had whipped back their blue wool capes, worked the wards, and done what was necessary. Everyone cooperated. Whole families were quarantined. And they did this willingly. "None of that mess about civil rights," they said. My father talked of ten-year-old Irish children who never got off Ellis Island. If they had consumption they were shipped back. People had signs on their doors, no one could work, leave the house, or go in. The plagues were conquered. How romantic, I remember thinking, a new disease.

For the next ten years I worked in many places. I cared for

cancer patients, head injury victims, prisoners. I was a traveling nurse, and went to rural Lousiana, rural New Mexico; the poor city neighborhoods of Savannah and San Antonio.

Then there were those first few mysterious deaths. I remember a young archaeology professor in Florida, beautiful features, tall and graceful body. He had developed an unusually aggressive lymphoma. None of the traditional things were helping. His glands were monstrous and painful. For six months he stayed in the hospital with no explanation, then he died. I remember changing his sheets often because of his night sweats. I rubbed his back, soaked and rubbed his feet, held him once when he cried. After a few years we would remember him as one of the first AIDS cases we had seen, but then he was just a man, thrown into a shadowy place where the body refused to behave, where each day there was one more new thing: back pain, a yeast infection, delirium.

I have a recruitment poster for World War II nurses. A woman is suspended in the air. She looks a lot like Marilyn, long shapely legs and a thigh-high white uniform. Her blonde hair is swept up and she stands wrapped in the American flag with planes buzzing around her and camouflaged tanks beneath her feet. She has her left arm raised in victory. It seems clear to me that in fighting TB and polio, the tactics we employed were much like those used to win World War II battles. My father escaped Germany after being shot down almost eighty miles behind enemy lines. He had memorized roads that were unoccupied, he knew where the enemy camps were. There were zones, there were parameters. Fighting AIDS is much more like Vietnam. There is chaos. The virus waits in ambush. Its form is unclear, it may even be a village child.

Enter Luis, my life teacher. It is now just two weeks since his death. There are no words to adequately describe his suffering.

His right eye was obliterated by a pear-sized sarcoma, purple vessels raised up and intractable. His left eye was infected with cytomegalovirus, an opportunistic infection that can cause blindness. If he tilted his head just right he could make out the blurred edge of you. His bones were pressing to break through his skin, and he had a large, water-filled penis that curved and changed color. It was his body, but most of the time he transcended it.

One day when we were sitting together talking, he mentioned how troubled he was that I never knew him when he was well. He used to be different, he told me. "I liked Judy Garland records," he said, "and other things: the beach, wearing hats, I have lots of hats; and I like to cook, I was never careless with cooking. I would take onions, tomatoes, or sage and cut them into small perfect pieces. Now I'm so tired, I just throw the whole thing in the pot. I wish you knew me then, when I had energy for cooking."

We spoke often of dying. He believed completely in heaven. He didn't know what it would be, but he knew Carlos, his spouse who had died of AIDS two years earlier, would be there. Once when Luis was being admitted to the hospital for fever, we spotted a decoration in the elevator. "I really want to live until Christmas," he said, "but I don't think I will." I took the shiny snowflake down, and put it under his blanket. Later, we hung it from the lamp in his hospital room, where it caught the light from the window and made bright lines on the wall. He went home three days later, lived until December 28th, when he gathered his family around him, asked their forgiveness for giving up, and died. His brother Edwin called and said, ironically, that he hadn't suffered, just went to sleep.

I have a photo he gave to me when I visited his home a few days before he died. He is leaning against a white stucco wall in Puerto Rico, his hair thick and black. In the background Carlos turns from the water's edge, and waves. There is so much sun, he is squinting. If you didn't know the color of his eyes you would have to guess, even in the photo, the love they have for each other connects through the sunlight in an arc over the water.

I wish I could know that this was a unique event. That for someone to suffer the way he did for two years was something I would never witness again. But with AIDS it is already untrue. The young hearts and lungs do not give up easily. The young lives hang on. There is a tremendous burden on the health care workers who manage and deliver home care. Home is where many AIDS patients die. City hospitals are overwhelmed by the needs of the drug-addicted who are infected. There are the suffering families, who struggle to keep their loved ones with them, despite economic devastation. These situations are frequently compounded by the fact that many of the caretakers are themselves HIV-positive. There are babies being born infected, many with no one to care for them or hold them.

This is what I also want you to understand. For the most part, in the midst of these realities of the illness, the spirits of the afflicted soar. In the clinic, one who is weak but still eating will give a hand to another, or offer hints on how to stop losing weight. There is a community of loss.

The virus has altered us all. Everyone is wounded and permanently changed. Those of us who watch closely know this: in their last nights they dream triumphantly, they have the old health back. They run in their sleep, or make love. There is a stretching out in sleep of their bodies, a relaxed curve to the shape of their bodies, their arms in sleep circle the missing loved ones.

In the Morgan Library, I stand before the illuminated manuscript, "Woman Clothed with the Sun." Beneath her feet, cherubs with blue and gold ribbons lift the air that holds her. She is in a circle of ascension. How like her I have felt. Their love has so altered me. I have known their spirits, which sometimes made me heavier, but mostly it was bright air that entered and lifted me up.

There is a clarity to the world now. In my home I notice the bulge of narcissus, the black spider in the white tub, a precarious web in the shower's corner.

I understand the fear that surrounds this disease. When I worked nights I would get phone calls from people worried because a friend who is HIV-positive had used their towels or taken water from their glass. I would tell them about how difficult it is for the virus to move from one person to another, what body fluids it travels in, what it takes to spread it. I talked of small gestures of comfort that are safe: kisses, hugs, spreading a blanket across the feet of the loved one. How fearless they could be, even in the room where one is dying, how I hoped they would think about the soul, and just before leaving the room lay a hand on the sick one, in blessing.

In leaning closer to one another during this epidemic, we may move beyond all the old thinking of isolation. This is the hard work of love.

LOOSE RIDER

Tory Dent

Tory Dent was born in 1958. She is the author of a book of poems, *What Silence Equals,* and has published poetry and art criticism in many periodicals, including *The Paris Review, Agni, The Kenyon Review, Arts, Flash Art, Parachute,* and *The Partisan Review.* She lives in New York City.

.... It was a typical winter non-day when I sat on the secondhand loveseat in my living room, draped with flowered English quilts eight times the value of the sofa itself in effort to reconfigure the stained and sullied condition of its firsthand life. I sat on the edge of the secondhand loveseat to be exact, perched with the receiver of a teal blue Princess phone (a color never to be carried again by Bell) in my hand. A curt snow flurry created static in the window like a TV program interrupted by emergency testing. I focused alternately on the flakes, then the gray infinitude of their insipid atmosphere in an effort to steady myself. It had been two weeks since I'd taken the test and today I would find out the results. I'd been put on hold by my doctor's secretary.

"Tory?"

"Dr. Mather."

"How are you?" he asks ceremoniously.

"Okay. And you?" I volley back, my anxiety starting to spike with this politesse. The teal blue receiver slips slightly in my perspiring hand.

"Okay." A brief omission. The tentative beat weighs heavily in my larynx.

"Well?" I ask with non-sequential agitation, my voice loud and throaty.

"It's inconclusive. You need to take the test again." I feel a sudden headache of confusion and sense of depression from the anticlimax.

"I don't understand."

"The test is inconclusive. You need to take it again," he said again, not robotically, not emotively. I'm straining to analyze what might be unspoken in these words: his tone of voice, the words themselves, his inflection.

"I don't understand," I repeat like a canary with a childlike sense of desperation and helplessness augmenting my confusion. I didn't expect this answer. Utilizing my unusual capacity for magical thinking I prepared myself for only one answer: *neative*, navigating the outcome by virtue of this preparation, naturally.

"It's inconclusive. You need to take the test again," he repeats, this time with more emotion than robotism. We went on then in this way for about ten more minutes, rather like that famous Abbott and Costello routine, "Who's on First?"

"I still don't understand."

"It's inconclusive. You have to take the test again."

"What does 'inconclusive' mean?"

"Inconclusive."

"But what does it mean?"

"It means the test was inconclusive. You have to take it again."

"Why do I have to take it again?"

"Because the test was inconclusive!" At this point we are both trying to make ourselves very clear. In other words, we're starting to raise our voices.

"*What* does inconclusive *mean?*" I ask—er—strongly.

"It *means* that the *test* is *inconclusive!*" He's definitely shouting at me now.

"But *what* does *that* mean? What *does* that *mean?* What . . . does . . . the . . . word . . . *inconclusive* . . . mean, *pre-cise-ly?*" I'm speaking now in a crisp and bitchy staccato. I've taken on this superior, bitter tone to counteract his shouting, to catch him on the short, as it were. It works.

"It means . . ." he draws in a long breath, and pauses, "it means that they screwed up the test. They didn't get a result. You have to take it again."

"They botched the test?" I feel a renewed vigor with this information.

"Yes," he confirms now quietly, almost funereally, sounding defeated. "You *have* to take the test again, Tory," he adds with paternal, adamantine authority.

"I don't *want* to take the test again," I retort, trying not to sound as bratty as I'm sure I sound. "I've changed my mind," I continue somewhat haughtily, becoming more the willful woman than the recalcitrant child.

"You *must* take the test again, Tory." His dark insistence unnerves me completely.

"*Why?*" I query, no beats skipped, nonplussed as if the topic were brought up for the first time out of the blue. "Why should I take this test? What will happen anyway? What would you do?" AZT was an experimental drug then. There was nothing doctors could do.

"We'll watch you." This sudden introduction of the royal *we* capped it off.

"Watch me, then!" I goaded him in final staccato starkness. There was silence on the other end and I said nothing. After a moment he beseeched me one more time to take the test and I declined again, this time with more grace, more akin to a ball belle turning down a dancing partner, regrettably, offering up her overbooked card as evidence of her regret. I'd changed my mind as if my hands were tied. I placed the teal blue receiver slowly back into its cradle and stared at the ensemble, pondering the scene that had taken place two weeks earlier the way one stares into a pool of water, for respite, for reverie, for reconsideration.

"Don't worry, Tory, it'll be negative." My doctor had smiled reassuringly, as I lay down on the examining table of his office on that February afternoon, three weeks before my thirtieth birthday. Deft with the needle, we let the small sucking sounds of tube after tube filling up with my blood take up the space of our unfounded anxiety. There was no risk group. There were no statistics. There wasn't a clue in the world that I would ever test positive. He touched my back with an extra pat of confidence, beyond the protocol of bedside manner yet within the confines of impeccable professionalism. This is a doctor's compassion. It is rare like a found object, and like a found object hard to detect at first its value. It cannot succeed alone in practice, and yet brilliant doctors are rendered impotent without it. Like playing "This Little Piggy Went to Market," a roster of doctors were about to make their debut, and star-studded it was at that. There would be the doctor who . . . and there would be the doctor that . . . and this was the doctor sent, like a sponger into a nuclear power plant, unto me with the news of my diagnosis. I never saw him again.

In those days the blood had to be hand-delivered. I volunteered to go myself since the office was short on staff that day. I remember staring at the tubes, dark and ruby-iridescent in my lap on the way down in the cab. I literally held my fate in my hands and I knew it. A strong feeling, an instinct, almost a voice, like a horse broken loose from its corral, its blanket askew on its furry back, its matted hair flaying in the musky

moorlike sky, wild with instinct, furious fear and clarity: I want
to throw the tubes away. I had changed my mind about taking
the test. I wanted to tell the cab driver my home address, crazy
me, you know women, so predisposed to whim and mood,
always changing their minds at the last minute. But I did nothing. I behaved mechanically, getting out in the cold air in front
of the Health Department, carrying the tubes in a brown paper
bag like some wacky off-the-wall drug dealer so hard up she's
pushing her own blood. I hurried inside with a hyper-awareness
of my actions as if witnessing myself through the vantage point
of astral projection: young woman in long black coat on black
and white tiles, head darting about like a blue jay's; you can see
her breath even inside it's so cold. I walked into what appeared
to be the lab that looked more like a large, institutional kitchen
with a table and cabinets on either side and one regular, rec-
tangular refrigerator, solitary as a snowman, in the alcove. A tall
and overweight Afro-American woman wearing yellow latex
rubber gloves responded with an exhausted and begrudging "In
there" and pointed with a yellow latex index finger to the refrigerator when I asked where should I put the blood. I opened the
door and placed the parcel in utter emptiness, on a freezing
metal rack amidst the other empty freezing metal racks. The
fluorescent tube lit the brown paper from the back so that it
became momentarily transparent like parchment and I could
see the vials one more time, a kind of postmodern sacrifice, a
kind of goodbye.

"Close the door," said the same monotone exhausted voice,
slightly more begrudging this time.

"Will it be all right?" I asked frantically, stupidly, my anxiety pitched to a fireball inside my stomach, so that the whole
scene had become entirely surreal with this final transaction of
hearing my voice, small and high and stupid echo inside this
not-quite-lab, this not-quite-kitchen, this not-quite-hallway;
steaming with cold like rapids of dry ice; this hot/cold,

black/white striptease of reality that smelled of rubbing alcohol: my black coat, my white skin, her white lab coat, her black skin, the black and white tiles, the yellow latex gloves, my dark, ruby-iridescent blood. She simply shook her head with annoyance and finished cleaning the table with a nondescript rag. I would find no compensation, no comfort in asking her more questions like "Will you make sure it's not lost?" "Will you make sure it's not mixed up with someone else's?" like babies in a hospital. I wanted to take her into brief confidentiality, tell her the Cliff Notes version of my life, perhaps over a cup of coffee. I wanted her to look after my blood like a guardian angel, a fairy godmother, and ensure that the results be negative. She continued to clean indifferently and I turned mechanically away, my step quickening a few paces from the refrigerator as if deeds were designed with a drive to complete themselves and we were merely their envoys. . . .

SPECIMEN DAYS

―――――――――――――――・――――――――――――――

Robert Massa

Robert Massa died of AIDS in 1994 at the age of 37. He first wrote about
the disease for *The Village Voice* in 1983. In 1987, he became founding editor of *The Body Positive*, a monthly newsletter for people who had tested
HIV-positive, and in 1990 Mr. Massa received a New York Foundation for
the Arts Fellowship for nonfiction literature.

I don't know where to go as I leave the doctor's office. The
shops and people seem two-dimensional. Sounds are muffled. I
keep thinking: pay attention to what you feel. But all I feel is
the wind.

I remember the museum is close by. The heavy woodwork,
the leaded windows, the cavernous rooms remind me of elementary school. I head up the central staircase, following the
path where the stone has been worn down by footsteps.

I'm impressed as always by the dinosaur bones. They are
displayed in action—about to fight, about to feed.

A tour guide breaks my thoughts. She tells a group of
schoolchildren to ignore the signs in the glass cases; natural history is advancing so rapidly, she explains, that the curators can't
keep up, and some of the information is out of date.

I'm disappointed to think that our science will someday seem quaint and that I'll never know what really happened to the dinosaurs.

We walk into a glassed-in sidewalk café near Dupont Circle. I make it a point to sit across from Daniel because I want to flirt without the others noticing. We talk about how the rest of the world seems so little aware of what we are going through and how much the neighborhood has changed. We order omelettes; I look around and realize it is lunchtime for the other customers.

Daniel has been traveling in the Midwest and says he's impressed by how close-knit gay people seem in small towns; he would trade some of the freedom we have in New York for that sense of community. We start to play the game, staring a bit too long, jerking our attention away. He apologizes for using Sweet 'n Low, and I confess I use too much salt. I look through the glass and say Washington might be a nice place to live after all.

Then I knock my fork on the floor and bend down to pick it up, but I'm not watching and I slam my forehead on the next table. It's quiet all around us. I look up to say, "I'm fine," but before I get the words out I see two drops of my blood, bright red against the white linen.

I drive to the suburbs to visit my father in the hospital. My hometown seems too manicured, like those model towns we used to build for the train set. My father's room is in a new wing of the hospital, with drop ceilings, Sheetrock walls, and a small crucifix over every door.

My mother and brother are there. I tell them Dad looks good and my mother smiles. I begin to resent the attention he's getting.

Later, I am alone with my father when he wakes up. We

have small talk. Suddenly, he asks if people still get AIDS from transfusions. I'm startled just to hear him say the word. I want to tell him I understand how afraid and alone he feels, but I'm not ready for him to know about me. I tell him to not worry—they screen blood now. He doesn't look convinced, but puts his head back and drifts off to sleep. I touch his hand and notice how much our fingers are alike.

A few weeks later he's back home and I visit him again. He seems small and hunched over, but the quickness is back in his eyes. He gives me a key to a safe-deposit box; his will and some savings bonds are inside. If anything happens to him, it's up to me to take care of the arrangements. I'm the only one who would be calm enough to know what to do.

I follow Peter out to the beach. Children from the village play off in the distance. The sun is already strong. Peter sits at the water's edge and lowers his head. I sit a few feet away, wondering what to say. It was easier back in the city; here there is too much time to think. I look back at the guest house and notice again how shabby it's gotten.

I touch his shoulder. He doesn't want to die alone. He doesn't want to die. I tell him I understand, I'm going through it too. That doesn't calm him. He starts up again, telling me how his friend died. I turn away.

Further down the beach, someone has sculpted a life-size person in the sand. The arms are crossed over the chest like a body in a casket. The face is peaceful. I start to tell Peter I heard these sculptures are part of an old folk religion still practiced on the island, but halfway through, I can't remember if that's true or I imagined it.

Suddenly, I envy his hysteria. I tell him that the frightened boy inside of him is the part I love most and that I would be there if he got sick. He calms down. We decide to go for a swim. The water's too cool and the tide's coming in, but we make it past where the waves are breaking and soak in the sun and the salt and the motion. When we return to land, the sand corpse has been washed away.

I'm making every effort to keep up my friendship with Tom. He's a connection to the days when everything was possible. Now that I've moved in with Peter, I worry that Tom may get lonely. And I know he's attracted to Peter. He doesn't hide his jealousy, and I don't hide that I enjoy it.

But tonight he's in one of his moods, smoking cigarettes between every course. He called to tell a friend about another friend and that friend told him about someone else. He's thinking of taking antidepressants, but he's afraid they'll suppress his immune system.

Tom starts describing how he's stopped going to memorials because they make him think about his own. I lean back, signal the waiter to bring the check, and say: "Don't worry, Tom. We're not planning to give you a memorial." I look into his face to see if he's amused, but see only anger and surprise. It's my turn, but he won't let me pay for dinner.

Peter complains that I go to ACT UP demos just to cruise. I tell him I go for the sense of event. But today, in front of the Stock Exchange, the rain has muffled the protesters. I'm watching from under the canopy of the Federal Building across the street, listening to a homeless man explain the scene to his companion.

Then I see Mark. I slip around the nearest column, hoping he hasn't seen me. I remember reading in *Alumni News* that he's a vice-president now. I'm embarrassed by my backpack and blue jeans. I tell myself he wouldn't be surprised to run into me here. He must have suspected me back in college.

I feel a tap on my shoulder and I spin around and Mark's smiling at me, extending his hand. As we're talking, I notice his eyes darting over to the demonstrators. I ask about his wife.

Beth had a miscarriage last summer, he says softly, but they're trying again now. Then he leans toward me, whispers, "Be happy," and disappears into the revolving door.

I'm staring into a shop window when I see a familiar face in the glass. David. We smile. Six years? Seven? You're looking good, he says, by which we both know he means healthy. What's new?

I don't know what to say. David and I had never gotten to know each other well. I throw out disjointed facts. New boyfriend, same job. And you?

David tested positive last week.

I reach over and put my arms around him. That's not like me. In those weeks we slept together so long ago, we never touched in the street.

At last I would meet the extended family. Easter is a major Greek holiday, so there would be plenty of ritual to get us through the evening. Peter's mother puts out a spread of lamb, spinach pie, and honey pastries. We crack open eggs dyed red in honor of Mary Magdalene and make wishes for the coming year. The older aunt never looks me in the eye, but sweet Aunt Kattina nods and smiles at me all through dinner. Later, the men laugh and argue over coffee while Peter and I help the women in the kitchen.

When we return home, Peter lights candles and we make love. Then he turns to the wall and we curl around each other. We will sleep with the window open because it's almost spring. I lie still, waiting to hear him snore.

In the middle of the night, Peter cries out and I wake him and say it was just a dream, go back to sleep. We lie back. I look down at my body, thinking that all we are is inside our skin, but in this moment that thought doesn't frighten me.

·

I'm tying up the newspapers. That's become my job. Peter is mopping, singing along with the music. The apartment smells like lemons and ammonia.

Then I spot Michael's obit. I quickly shuffle it to the bottom of the pile, wondering if Peter knows. I decide to wait for the right moment to tell him.

But later, when I'm emptying the trash, I discover he's already removed Michael's card from the Rolodex.

I notice a slight awkwardness in my step. After a brain scan and biopsy, I'm told I have a brain infection, which the AIDS treatment handbook I pull down from my shelf describes as "largely untreatable, rapidly progressive, and fatal."

Peter is scrubbing the turkey, twisting his face in disgust as he slaps the gizzards into the sink. Carol is rolling pie crusts, explaining the virtues of shortening over real butter. The cats hover wide-eyed in the doorway. Sage, rosemary, and lots of thyme, I remember my grandmother telling me as she violently shook the spice can over the bowl of stuffing. Peter's mother bursts in, and they argue in Greek until he lets her peel the apples.

Later, my family comes. It's the first time I've seen them since the news, and they sit across the table in their best clothes, huddled together, motionless and grim like the Romanovs waiting for their executioners. My niece crawls over and sits in my lap.

I sit in the dark corner, wanting to get up to respond to the man who's rubbing his crotch in my face, afraid to lose my seat. I rub saliva from my hand and reach up to touch a passing nipple. I've convinced myself the sex club is one of the places I feel safest. The corridors are too narrow and crowded for me to fall. It's so dark, no one seems to notice the way I move, or maybe they think I'm just drunk. I've learned something about myself coming here: The fun was always in the chase.

I'm strapped to a table wearing a blue paper gown with a plastic cage around my head, being slid into the scanner. They shut the hatch, so I am completely enclosed, like an astronaut. The test lasts longer than I expect; I'm wondering if that's a good sign. They pipe in music to drown out the distant jackhammer rumble of the scan. I had brought CDs—Bach and a pop song that reminds me of Peter—but when they ask what kind of music I prefer, I just want to get it over with and I say I don't care. So they pipe in the radio. It's rush hour, so I lie there listening to anxious traffic updates.

We're in a damp East Village basement, watching a play about nuclear holocaust. Strobe lights, screeching punk music, eager actors stumbling around with red Jello dripping from their cheeks. Later, in front of the theater, the lead walks by, without his makeup. He has a lesion on his face.

Peter yells, "Snap out of it," complaining that my walk—dragging my left foot, my left arm curled up in front of me like a beggar—"looks like something out of Dickens." He's mad at my family today, after a message from my brother the priest informing us that I had upset my sister because I sounded "down" on the phone. I think back to the day two months ago, my birthday, that I told her, as she returned home from the butcher, watching while she slapped fistfuls of chopped meat into burgers, wrapping each with both Saran and foil to protect them. When I told my brother the night before, he described Pascal's wager—that we might as well believe in God, because we'll be better off if he exists and no worse off if he doesn't. I told him I didn't think God's so easily fooled.

I never wanted to open gifts on Christmas, because when the

boxes were all unwrapped, it was over. This year, I'm having trouble tearing the paper, so I just want to get through it quickly. We usually buy a tree that's much too big for the room, but this year we buy a small one we can replant in the spring.

I lie on the couch, thinking I should be reading Proust or sailing to Tahiti, strategizing whether to get up to go to the bathroom or hold it till Peter gets home. Suddenly, the roofers start to lift the skylight, two days ahead of schedule. A few flakes of snow fall into the room, sprinkling my blanket like sugar. I pretend to be asleep because I don't want it to stop.

PORNOGRAPHY

Richard McCann

Richard McCann's fiction and poetry have appeared in *The Atlantic,* *Esquire, Ploughshares,* and in numerous anthologies, including *The Penguin Book of Gay Short Stories.* He has received numerous honors and awards, including fellowships from the MacDowell Colony, Yaddo, and the Fine Arts Work Center in Provincetown. He is the author of *Nights of 1990* and *Dream of the Traveler* and a novel, *Mother.* He lives in Washington, D.C., where he co-directs the MFA Program in Creative Writing at The American University.

1.

Jean Genet once said—or so the story goes—that his greatest disappointment as a writer was that he set out to create pornography but it became art.

As a poet and fiction writer who attempts to write about AIDS—about the ways in which AIDS has altered one's relationship to desire, for instance, and to the body—I increasingly find myself writing about a sexuality I once practiced but about which I could not write. Nights in a field near an abandoned Luna Park outside Vicenza. Nights in the public toilets beneath the *Porta Nigra* in Trier, or nights in the washroom of the *Hauptbahnhof* in Wiesbaden. Drunken nights, by the back gate to the *Englischer Garten*. I could see a man in the distance, his trousers down around his ankles, waiting beneath a tree.

My regret is not the same as Genet's. My regret is that I took so long to write about my sexuality—even though it wasn't a choice I could make, at least not consciously—that my work, by the time I began it, had already taken the form of an elegy.

2.

My greatest disappointment is that I set out to make pornography but it became art.

But to turn this around, to derive a question from it, for the writer who sets out to make art: Does an art about AIDS require what has been thought of as pornographic?

Our lives, for instance, have been thought of as "pornographic."

Not long ago the poet Tony Hoagland, the author of *Sweet Ruin*, told me that he believed that gay male poets would need to redefine the form and meaning of the elegy.

Artist Karen Bermann, in *Theater of Operations:* "Upon the occasion of emission, the mouth itself is a violated border, an exit wound; sobs and exclamations may break from the mouth as the utterance . . . tears its way out."

I would like to see the elegy that is an "exit wound"; the elegy of anger, even rage; the elegy that could include the pornographic.

Like these lines from Mark Doty's "Tiara," a poem whose meditative and elegiac grace rises from anger:

And someone said he asked for it.
Asked for it—when all he did
was go down into the salt tide

of wanting as much as he wanted,
giving himself over so drunk
or stoned it almost didn't matter who . . .

Or these lines, from James White's "Taken to a Room":

I pant hard over this poem
wanting to write your body again.

To "pant hard" in the act of sexual passion, of masturba-
tion; to "pant hard" with the work of making the poem. Wasn't
that the work of pornography, as Genet said he saw it?– The
body you still longed for, resurrected before you again . . .

Genet, the pornographer, so inexpert at narrative; Genet,
whose characters resembled shrines . . .

3.

Pornography, as defined by the *American Heritage Dictionary*:
"Written, graphic or other forms of communication intended
to excite lascivious feelings . . ."

A question for Jean Genet: At what point does pornography
become art?

On Pearl Harbor Day, 1984, my lover was told he was HIV-
positive. He called me from Sacramento, where he'd gotten sick
on a business trip, to tell me the news.

For a long time afterwards, I couldn't watch porn films,
although I had often enjoyed them. For a long time I felt as if
those perfect bodies–those gym bodies, those bodies on which
even the idiosyncratic irregularities of pubic hair had been
"repaired," "improved," "cosmeticized"–now contained some
message about death.

As what body does not?

They were mortal, after all: those "gay bodies," those
achievements of the late 1970s and early '80s; those bodies that

seemed sculpted from marble, those bodies that seemed as if they could defeat everything, including personality and time. As Edmund White writes in "Esthetics and Loss": "the body that until recently was at once so natural (athletic, young, casually dressed) and so artificial (pumped up, pierced, ornamented) . . ."

But that body no longer existed. Now the body seemed a door to grief.

Dinner party chatter, circa 1986: "Don't you hate it when you can see that the actors in porn films are wearing *condoms?*" As if one couldn't bear to be reminded.

A few years later, one couldn't bear to see the actors without condoms. One was always thinking, "AIDS, AIDS, AIDS, AIDS."

Does pornography become art when it reminds you of that of which you cannot bear to be reminded?

If that was the case, pornography itself no longer existed.

4.

My earliest pornography: the medical photos of naked men in my sister-in-law's nursing textbook. The man whose chest and stomach were puckered with burn scars. The man whose trunk and legs were bruised with syphilitic lesions. The man with scoliosis, lateral curvature of the spine.

But sometimes, if I looked closely, I could see the shadowy darkness of their genitalia, the clefts of their exposed buttocks. Perhaps I learned how to love these men for what I could salvage from them, in parts. This man, with his thick pale penis, mysterious foreskin. This man, whose long penis grazed the inside of his thigh.

"Forms of communication intended to excite lascivious feelings . . ." But what was I required to exclude, in order to excite myself?

I jerked off into a Kleenex. I buried the Kleenex in the trash.

Dinner party chatter, circa 1993: "Should video porn include only scenes of 'safer sex'? Have you seen *Hispanic Homeboys?*"

As for me: I've lost my taste for historical romances. If I were Derek Jarman, I'd remake *The Decameron* as he made *Edward II,* in modern dress. Boccaccio, with dental dams and rainbow-colored rubbers. (The porn star Scott O'Hara: "I want to make gay porn starring actors with AIDS.")

Yesterday a friend was telling me about a radio broadcast she had heard. A gay man, a former Mormon, was telling how he had confessed to his bishop that he had "stimulated himself" by looking at pictures of naked men.

In the future, when you think of a man's naked body, the bishop had advised him, *I want you to imagine it covered with a huge wound.*

"Isn't that awful?" my friend asked.

Yes, it is awful, I thought. *I know what that bishop is getting at. He means to do violence to the body.*

But it was hard not to think of Julia Kristeva's "Approaching Abjection": "A wound with blood and pus, or the sickly acrid smell of sweat, of decay, does not signify death. In the presence of signified death—a flat encephalograph, for instance—I would understand, react, or accept. No, as in true theater, without makeup or masks, refuse and corpses show me what I permanently thrust aside in order to live. These body fluids, this defilement, this shit are what life withstands, hardly and with difficulty, on the part of death. There, I am at the border of my condition as a living being."

It is hard not to think of Edmund White: "The other day I saw stenciled on a Paris wall an erect penis, its dimensions included in centimeters, and the words *Faut Pas Rêver* (You mustn't dream)."

I pant hard over this poem/wanting to write your body again.

Dear body; dearest one, whom I still miss:

At night you straddled my hips and rose above me. You stroked your cock across my face, my mouth. You came.

It was dark. You wrote your name on my bare chest.

I'LL BE SOMEWHERE LISTENING FOR MY NAME

Melvin Dixon

Melvin Dixon died of AIDS-related complications in the fall of 1992. He published two novels, *Vanishing Rooms* and *Trouble the Water,* and a volume of poetry, *Change of Territory.* He translated *The Collected Poems of Leopold Sedar Senghor* and received fellowships in poetry and fiction from the National Endowment for the Arts and the New York Arts Foundation. His work has appeared in many journals and anthologies, including *Men on Men 2, Best New Gay Fiction, Poets for Life: 76 Poets Respond to AIDS, Brother to Brother,* and *In the Life.*

> *When He calls me, I will answer*
> *When He calls me, I will answer*
> *When He calls me, I will answer*
> *I'll be somewhere listening for my name*
> *I'll be somewhere listening*

As gay men and lesbians, we are the sexual niggers of our society. Some of you may have never before been treated like a second-class, disposable citizen. Some of you have felt a certain privilege and protection in being white, which is not to say that others are accustomed to or have accepted being racial niggers, and feel less alienated. Since I have never encountered a person of no color, I assume that we are all persons of color. Like fashion victims, though, we are led to believe that some colors are more acceptable than others, and those acceptable colors have been so endowed with universality and desirability that the color hardly seems to exist at all—except, of course, to those who are of a different color and pushed outside the rainbow. My own fantasy is to be locked inside a Benetton ad.

No one dares call us sexual niggers, at least not to our faces. But the epithets can be devastating or entertaining: We are faggots and dykes, sissies and bulldaggers. We are funny, sensitive, Miss Thing, friends of Dorothy, or men with "a little sugar in the blood," and we call ourselves what we will. As an anthropologist/linguist friend of mine calls me in one breath, "Miss Lady Sister Woman Honey Girl Child."

Within this environment of sexual and racial niggerdom, recovery isn't easy. Sometimes it is like trying to fit a size-twelve basketball player's foot into one of Imelda Marcos's pumps. The color might be right, but the shoe still pinches. Or, for the more fashionable lesbians in the audience, lacing up those combat boots only to have extra eyelets staring you in the face, and you feel like Olive Oyl gone trucking after Minnie Mouse.

As for me, I've become an acronym queen: BGM ISO same or other. HIV plus or minus. CMV, PCP, MAI, AZT, ddl, ddC. Your prescription gets mine.

Remember those great nocturnal emissions of your adolescent years? They told us we were men, and the gooey stuff proved it. Now in the nineties, our nocturnal emissions are night sweats, inspiring fear, telling us we are mortal and sick, and that time is running out.

In my former neighborhood in Manhattan, I was a member of the 4H Club: the Happy Homosexuals of Hamilton Heights. Now it is the 3D Club: the dead, the dying, those in despair. I used to be in despair; now I'm just dying.

I come to you bearing witness to a broken heart; I come to you bearing witness to a broken body—but a witness to an unbroken spirit. Perhaps it is only to you that such witness can be brought and its jagged edges softened a bit and made meaningful. We are facing the loss of our entire generation. Lesbians lost to various cancers, gay men lost to AIDS. What kind of witness will you bear? What truthtelling are you brave enough to utter and endure the consequences of your unpopular message?

Last summer my lover Richard died. We had been lovers for twelve years. His illness and death were so much a part of my illness and life that I felt that I, too, had died. I'm just back from Florida, visiting his family and attending the unveiling of his headstone. Later this month, our attorney will file the necessary papers for the settling of Richard's estate, and I shall return to our summer home in Provincetown without him, but not without the rich memories of our many years there. And he is everywhere inside me listening for his name.

I've lost Richard, I've lost vision in one eye, I've lost the contact of people I thought were friends, I've lost the future tense from my vocabulary, I've lost my libido, and I've lost more weight and appetite than Nutri-System would want to claim.

My life is closing. Oh, I know all the clichés: "We all have to die" and "Everything comes to an end." But when is an ending a closure and when does closure become a new beginning? Not always. It is not automatic. We have to work at it. If an end is termination, closure involves the will to remember, which gives new life to memory.

As creators, we appear to strike a bargain with the immortality we assume to be inherent in art. Our work exists outside us and will have a life independent of us. Doris Grumbach, in her recent book, *Coming into the End Zone,* reminds us of the life of books: "Let the book make its own way, even through the thick forest of competitors, compelling readers by the force of its words and its vision."

I am reminded of a poignant line from George Whitmore, who struck a Faustian bargain with AIDS: If he wrote about it, perhaps he wouldn't get it. George, as you know, lost that battle, but his books are still with us. His two novels are *The Confessions of Danny Slocum* and *Nebraska*. His harrowing reporting on AIDS is called *Someone Was Here*. And now George is somewhere listening for his name, hearing it among us.

I am not above bargaining for time and health. And I am troubled by the power of prophecy inherent in art. One becomes afraid to write because one's wildest speculations may in fact come true. I wrote all the AIDS poems published in Michael Klein's *Poets for Life* before I knew I was HIV-positive. I was responding in part to my sense of isolation and helplessness as friends of mine fell ill. And when I published the poem "And These Are Just a Few" in the *Kenyon Review,* I made a point of acknowledging the dead and those yet fighting for life. I'm sorry to report that of the twenty people mentioned in the poem, only two are presently alive.

As writers, we are a curious lot. We begin our projects with much apprehension about the blank page. But then as the material assumes its life, we resist writing that last stanza or paragraph. We want to avoid putting a final period to it all. Readers are no better. We all want to know what new adventures await Huck Finn or if Ishmael finally "comes out" following his "marriage" with QueeQueg. As sequels go, I'm not sure the world needed Ripley's extension to *Gone with the Wind,* but consider *Rocky 10,* in which the son of the erstwhile fighter discovers he is gay and must take on the arch-villain Harry Homophobia. Would the title have to be changed to *Rockette?*

Then there is the chilling threat of erasure.

Gregory, a friend and former student of mine, died last fall. On the day following a memorial service for him, we all were having lunch and laughing over our fond memories of Greg and his many accomplishments as a journalist.

Suddenly his lover had a shock. He had forgotten the remaining copies of the memorial program in the rental car he had just returned. Frantic to retrieve the programs, which had Greg's picture on the cover and reprints of his autobiographical essays inside, his lover called the rental agency to reclaim the material. They had already cleaned the car, but he could come out there, they said, and dig through the dumpster for whatever he could find. Hours later, the lover returned empty-handed, the paper programs already shredded, burned, and the refuse carted away. Greg had been cremated once again, but this time without remains or a classy urn to house them. The image of Greg's lover sifting through the dumpster is more haunting than the reality of Greg's death, for Greg had made his peace with the world. The world, however, had not made its peace with him.

His siblings refused to be named in one very prominent obituary, and Greg's gayness and death from AIDS were not to be mentioned at the memorial service. Fortunately, few of us heeded the family's prohibition. While his family and society may have wanted to dispose of Greg even after his death, some of us tried to reclaim him and love him again and only then release him.

I was reminded of how vulnerable we are as gay men, as black gay men, to the disposal or erasure of our lives.

But Greg was a writer, a journalist who had written on AIDS, on the business world, and on his own curious life journey from his birth in the poor Anacostia district of Washington, D.C., to scholarships that allowed him to attend Exeter and then Williams College and on to the city desks of our nation's most prominent newspapers. His words are still with us, even if his body and those gorgeous programs are gone. And Greg is somewhere listening for his name.

We must, however, guard against the erasure of our experience and our lives. As white gays become more and more prominent—and acceptable to mainstream society—they project a racially exclusive image of gay reality. Few men of color will ever be found on the covers of the *Advocate* or *New York Native*. As white gays deny multiculturalism among gays, so too do black communities deny multisexualism among its members. Against this double cremation, we must leave the legacy of our writing and our perspectives on gay and straight experiences.

Our voice is our weapon.

Several months ago the editors of *Lambda Book Report* solicited comments from several of us about the future of gay and lesbian publishing. My comments began by acknowledging my grief for writers who had died before they could make a significant contribution to the literature. The editors said my comments suggested a "bleak and nonexistent future" for gay publishing. Although I still find it difficult to imagine a glorious future for gay publishing, that does not mean I cannot offer some concrete suggestions to ensure that a future does exist.

First, reaffirm the importance of cultural diversity in our community. Second, preserve our literary heritage by posthumous publications and reprints, and third, establish grants and fellowships to ensure that our literary history is written and passed on to others. I don't think these comments are bleak, but they should remind us of one thing: We alone are responsible for the preservation and future of our literature.

If we don't buy our books, they won't get published. If we don't talk about our books, they won't get reviewed. If we don't write our books, they won't get written.

As for me, I may not be well enough or alive next year to attend the lesbian and gay writers conference, but I'll be somewhere listening for my name.

I may not be around to celebrate with you the publication of gay literary history. But I'll be somewhere listening for my name.

If I don't make it to Tea Dance in Provincetown or the

Pines, I'll be somewhere listening for my name.

You, then, are charged by the possibility of your good health, by the broadness of your vision, to remember us.

PUCK

Paul Monette

Paul Monette died of AIDS in February, 1995. He is the author of many books—poetry, fiction, and autobiography. His 1992 memoir, *Becoming a Man: Half a Life Story*, won the National Book Award. His most recent book of personal essays is *Last Watch of the Night*, where "Puck" also appears.

Stevie had been in the hospital about a week and a half, diagnosed with PCP, his first full-blown infection. For some reason he wasn't responding to the standard medication, and his doctors had put him on some new exotic combination regimen—one side effect of which was to turn his piss blue. He certainly didn't act or feel sick, except for a little breathlessness. He was still miles from the brink of death. Not even showing any sign of late-stage shriveling up—let alone the ravages of end stage, where all that's left of life is sleep shot through with delirium.

Stevie was reading the paper, in a larky mood because he'd just had a dose of Ativan. I was sitting by the window, doodling with a script that I had to finish quick in order to keep my insurance. "I miss Puck," he announced to no one in particular, no response required.

And I stopped writing and looked out the window at the

heat-blistered parking lot, the miasma of low smog bleaching the hills in the distance. "You think Puck's going to survive me?"

"Yup," he replied. Which startled me, a bristle of the old denial that none of us was going to die just yet. Even if we were all living our lives in "dog years" now, seven for every twelve-month, I still couldn't feel my own death as a palpable thing. To have undertaken the fight as we had for better drugs and treatment, such that we had become a guerrilla tribe of amateur microbiologists, pharmacist/shamans, our own best healers—there were those of us who'd convinced ourselves in 1990 that the dying was soon going to stop.

AIDS, you see, was on the verge of becoming a "chronic manageable illness." That was our totem mantra after we buried the second wave, or was it the third? When I met Steve Kolzak on the Fourth of July in '88, he told me he had seven friends who were going to die in the next six months—and they did. It was my job to persuade him that we could fall in love anyway, embracing between the bombs. And then we would pitch our tent in the chronic, managable clearing, years and years given back to us by the galloping strides of science. No more afflicted than a diabetic, the daily juice of insulin keeping him one step ahead of his body.

So don't tell me I had less time than a ten-year-old dog—admittedly one who was a specimen of roaring good health, still out chasing coyotes in the canyon every night, his watch-man's bark at home sufficient to curdle the blood. But if I was angry at Stevie for saying so, I kept it to myself as the hospital stay dragged on. A week of treatment for PCP became two, and he found himself reaching more and more for the oxygen. Our determination, or mine at least, to see this bout as a minor inconvenience remained unshaken. Stevie upped his Ativan and mostly retained his playful demeanor, though woe to the nurse or technician who thought a stream of happy talk would

get them through the holocaust. Stevie's bark was as lethal as
Puck's if you said the wrong thing.

And he didn't get better either, because it wasn't pneumonia that was killing him. I woke up late on Friday, the fifteenth
of September to learn they'd moved him to intensive care, and
I raced over to find him in a panic, fear glazing his flashing Irish
eyes as he clutched the oxygen cup to his mouth. They pulled
him through the crisis with steroids but still wouldn't say what
the problem was. Some nasty bug that a sewer of antibiotics
hadn't completely arrested yet. But surely all it required was a
little patience till one of these drugs kicked in.

His family arrived from back East, the two halves of the
divorce. Yet it looked as if the emergency had passed, thus the
false promise of massive steroids. But I mean he looked fine.
He was impish and animated all through the weekend; it was
we who had to be vigilant lest he get too tired. And I was so
manically certain that he'd pull through, I could hardly take it
in at first when one of the docs, shifty-eyed, refined the diagnosis: "He's having a toxic reaction to the chemo."

The chemo? But how could that be? They'd been treating
his KS for sixteen months, till all the lesions were under control. Even the ones on his face, you had to know they were
there to spot them under his beard, a scatter of faded purple.
Besides, KS wasn't a sickness really, it was mostly just a nui-
sance. This was how deeply invested I was in denial, the 1990
edition. Since KS had never landed us in the hospital, it didn't
count. And the chemo was the treatment, so how could it be
life-threatening?

Easily, as it turned out. The milligram dosage of bleomycin,
a biweekly drip in the doctor's office, is cumulative. After a certain point you run the risk of toxicity, your lungs seizing with
fibrous tissue—all the resilience gone till you can't even whistle
in the dark anymore. You choke to death the way Stevie did,
gasping into the oxygen mask, a little less air with every breath.

Still, there were moments of respite, even on that last day. "I'm not dying, am I?" he asked about noon, genuinely astonished. Finally his doctor came in and broke the news: the damage to the lungs was irreversible, and the most we could hope for was two or three weeks. Stevie nodded and pulled off the mask to speak. "Listen, I'm a greedy bastard," he declared wryly. "I'll take what I can get." As I recall, the idea was to send him home in a wheelchair with an oxygen tank.

I cried when the doctor left, trying to tell him how terrible it was, though he knew it better than I. Yet he smiled and put out a hand to comfort me, reassuring me that he felt no panic. He was on so much medication for pain and anxiety, his own dying had become a movie—a sad one, to be sure, but the Ativan-Percodan cocktail was keeping the volume down. I kept saying how much I loved him, as if to store the feeling up for the empty days ahead. Was there anything I could do? Anything left unsaid?

He shook his head, that muzzy wistful smile. Then his eyebrows lifted in surprise: "I'm not going to see Puck again." No regret, just amazement. And then it was time to grab the mask once more, the narrowing tunnel of air, the morphine watch. Twelve hours later he was gone, for death was even greedier than he.

And I was a widower twice now. Nothing for it but to stumble through the week that followed, force-fed by all my anguished friends, pulling together a funeral at the Old North Church at Forest Lawn. A funeral whose orations smeared the blame like dogshit on the rotting churches of this dead Republic, the politicians who run the ovens and dance on our graves. In the limo that took us up the hill to the gravesite, Steve's mother Dolores patted my knee and declared with a ribald trace of an Irish brogue: "Thanks for not burning the flag."

We laughed. A mere oversight, I assured her. She knew that Steve and I had spent a fruitless afternoon the previous Fourth

of July—our anniversary, as it happened—going from Thrifty to
Target trying to find stars-and-stripes to burn at our party. No
such luck: all the flags we found were plastic or polyester, more
or less the consistency of a cheap shower curtain. A perfect
symbol, we realized, of the country we had lost during the
decade of the calamity. So we'd had to forego the charred party
favors and made do with vituperation, sharing with our friends
over the weiners and potato salad a kind of Swiftian tirade
against the forces that gloated to see us die.

We buried the urn of his ashes high on a hill just at the rim
of the chaparral, at the foot of a California live oak. The long
shadow of our grieving circle fell across the hillside grass, where
a mere ten feet below I had buried Roger four years before. A
shadow that fell on my own grave, as a matter of fact, which is
just to the left of Roger's, as if I will one day fling an arm about
him and cradle us to sleep. After the putrefaction of the flesh,
a pair of skeletons tangled together like a couple of metaphysical lovers out of Donne. And my other bone-white arm reaching above my skull, clawing the six-foot dirt with piano-key
fingers, trying to get to Steve's ashes, just out of reach.

But what has it all got to do with the dog, exactly? My
friend Victor stayed with me for the first week of Widowhood
II, but when at last he went off to juggle the shards of his own
dwindling immunity, I woke to a smudged October morning.
And my first thought wasn't *Oh poor me*, about which I had
already written the book, but rather this: *Who's going to take care
of Puck?* Nudged perhaps by the beast himself, who sprawled
across the middle of the sagging double bed, permitting me a
modest curl of space on the far left side.

You must try to appreciate, I never used to be anything like
a rapturist about dogs, Puck or any other. Cesar used to say that
Puck was the only dog he knew who'd been raised without any
sentimentality at all. I was such a manic creature myself during
his formative years that it was all he could do to scramble out

of my lurching way, and not to take it personally when I'd shoo him away for no reason. This was not the same as having trained him. He rather tumbled up, like one of those squalling babies in Dickens, saved in the nick of time from a scald of boiling water by a harried Mrs. Micawber.

And yet when Roger died, and I thought I had died along with him, the only thing that got me out of bed, groggy at sunset, was that Puck still had to be fed. I could see in his limpid, heartstopping eyes that he knew Roger was not coming back, or maybe he just acquired a permanent wince to see me sobbing so unconsolably, hour after hour, gallantly putting his chin on the bed with a questioning look, in case I wanted company. I remember asking my brother in Pennsylvania if the dog could be shipped to him when I died, an event that seemed at the time as close as the walls of this room. But I didn't really like to think of Puck snuffling about in the fields of rural Bucks County, he whose breeding made him thrive in the desert hills around us.

Half Rhodesian ridgeback, half black lab—or half Zimbabwe ridgeback, I ought to say, one of my earliest encounters with political correctness having occurred in Laurel Canyon Park in the early eighties, a place where we could run our dogs off lead, one eye peeled for the panel truck of Animal Control. A sixty-dollar ticket if they caught you—or in this case, if they caught Puck, who left the paying of municipal fines in my capable hands.

He was one of a litter of nine, his mother a purebred ridgeback, tawny and noble, her back bisected by the stiff brush of her ridge, which ran from just behind her shoulders and petered out at her rump. A dog bred to hunt lions, we'd heard, especially prized for being able to go long stretches without any water, loping across the veldt. And as a sort of modulation of that terrifying bark, a bay of Baskerville proportions, the ridgeback had developed over time a growl as savage and indistinguishable as the lions it stalked. Try to get near a ridgeback when he's feeding, you'll see what I mean. You feel like one of those helpless children about to lose an arm through a chain-link rence, waving a box of Cracker Jacks in the roaring face of the king.

Ah but you see, there were compensating factors on the father's side. For Nellie, fertile mother of Puck and his eight siblings, had gotten it on with a strapping black lab high up in Benedict Canyon. A lab who was considered most déclassé, perhaps a bit of a half-breed himself, so friendly and ebullient that his people were always in peril of being knocked over or slobbered on. Not at all the genes that Nellie's owners were seeking to rarefy even further. We were told all this in a rush by Nellie's mistress, herself the achingly pretty daughter of a wondrously tucked and lifted movie star of the fifties—who looked like sisters if you squinted, beautiful and nothing else, the perfect ticket in L.A. to a long and happy journey on the median strip of life.

This was at a Thanksgiving supper in Echo Park—not the year we found the murdered Latino in the driveway as we left, but I think the year afterwards. In any case Roger and I had been worrying over the issue of a watchdog for some time now, as a security system cheaper by far than the alarm circuits that wired the hills around us, shrieking falsely into the night. The starlet daughter assured us ridgebacks were brilliant sentries, ferociously protective.

We went back and forth in the next few weeks, warned by both our families that it was just another thing to tie us down. Besides, we traveled too much, and it wasn't fair to an animal to be getting boarded all the time. None of them understood how stirred we'd been the previous spring, when a whimper brought us to the front door one stormy night. A bedraggled one-eyed Pekingese dripped on the tile, matted and scrawny and quaking in the rain. The most improbable creature, the very last dog that either of us would have chosen. But we couldn't send him back out in the whirlwind either, a bare hors d'oeuvre for the sleek coyotes that roamed our canyon in pairs.

We put signs on the trees up and down Kings Road, FOUND instead of the usual LOST, for cats especially disappeared with alarming frequency in the hills. Nobody called to claim the one-eyed runt, and it started to look as if we were stuck with him. Without consultation Roger began to call him Pepper and comb him out. I resisted mightily: *This was not by a long shot what anyone would call a watchdog.* I felt faintly ridiculous walking Pepper with his string leash on, as if I'd become an aging queen before my time. Thus I withheld my sentiments rigorously, leaving most of the care and feeding to Roger—though now and again I'd permit the orphan to perch on my lap while I typed.

And then about three weeks later we were strolling up Harold Way, Roger and Pepper and I, past the gates to Liberace's spread. We turned to a cry of delight, as a young black woman came running down the driveway. "Thass my mama dog," she squealed, scooping the one-eyed dustmop into her arms. In truth, Pepper seemed as overjoyed as she, licking her with abandon. The young woman called uphill to the kitchen yard, summoning her mother: "Grits home!" And a moment later an equally joyous woman came trundling towards us, crisp white uniform and billowing apron worthy of Tara.

No no, of course we wouldn't dream of taking money in return. This joyous reunion was all the reward we needed. And so trudged on home, trying not to feel even more ridiculous as we hastily put away the doll-size bowls by the kitchen door that had held Pepper/Grits's food and water. We laughed it off, or tried to anyway, gushing appropriately when the daughter appeared at our door that evening, bearing a peach pie almost too pretty to eat. "This is like Faulkner," Roger declared as we sliced the bounty. Faulkner, I replied, would not have used a Pekingese.

We never saw Pepper again—never even had the chance to ask how he'd lost that eye. But it goes to show how primed we were at the end of the year, when the starlet called nearly every day to say the litter was going fast. We thought we'd go over and have a look, but the only time the lot of us were free was Christmas morning. "Now we don't have to take one," I admonished Roger as we turned up the dirt road. A minute later we were in the kitchen, inundated by the scrambling of nine puppies. "Pick a lively one," I said, though the sheer explosion of canine anarchy didn't seem to have produced a sluggard or a runt. They squirmed out of our hands and yapped and chased. We couldn't have been said to have actually made a choice. The starlet and her human pups were waiting impatiently in the living room to open their gifts. Roger and I exchanged a shrug, and I reached for the one who was trying to crawl behind the refrigerator.

"You don't owe me anything," the starlet trilled. "Just the fifty bucks for his shots." We waved and promised to send a check, clambering into the car with our erupting bundle in tow. A black lab followed us barking down the drive. The father, we supposed. "He's not going to be *that* big, is he?" murmured Roger in some dismay. By the time we got home we were calling him Puck, in part because some friends of ours had just named a daughter Ariel, and we'd liked the Shakespearean spin of that, the sense that we were bringing home a changeling. The first thing Puck did when he tottered into the house was make for the Christmas tree, where he squatted and peed on a package from Gump's.

I don't remember a whole lot after that, not for the first five years, so assiduously was I trying to avoid the doggy sort of bathos. I do recall how fretful Roger was in the first six months, waiting for Puck to lift his leg to void instead of squatting. And the moment of triumph when he finally did, on a bush of wild anise. His main lair was beneath my butcher-block desk in the study—where he lies even as I write, his head propped uncomfortably on the wooden crossbeam that holds the legs in place. We quickly learned that he wouldn't be budged from any of his makeshift doghouses, which came to include the undercave of every table in the house. A lion's growl of warning if you got too close.

I fed him, I walked him. As I say, I was crazed in those years like a starlet myself, frantic to have a script made, fawning indiscriminately as a puppy over every self-styled producer who left a spoor in my path. I was so unbearably sophisticated, convinced I could reconfigure the Tracy/Hepburn magic, so glib and airy-fairy my shit didn't stink. For a time I even began to question my life with Roger and Puck both as perhaps being too bourgeois for words.

None of the scripts got made, of course. I was tossed on my ass as a loser and a failure, unable to get my calls returned, no matter how desperately I courted the assistants of assistants. I fell into a wrongheaded love affair with a hustler—literally the fifty-bucks-a-pop variety, which reminds me I never paid the debt to the starlet for Puck's shots, which would have been a lot better use of the money. Within a few weeks the hustler had sucked all my marrow and moved on. I careened through a year of near-breakdown, writing plays but mostly whining, and nearly drove Roger away in the process.

Yet we never stopped taking that evening walk, along the rim of the hill that led from Kings Canyon to Queens, Puck rooting ahead of us through the chaparral. I'm not quite sure how he managed to serve two masters, but was clearly far too well-bred to choose sides. We simply represented different orbits, centered of course on him. I was the one who sat at the desk while he slept at my feet all day, and Roger the one who came home at six, sending him into paroxysms of excited barking. The late-night walk was a threesome, no hierarchy of power. I'm not saying it kept Roger and me together, all on its own, but the evening stroll had about it a Zen calm—so many steps to the bower of jacarandas at Queens Road, so many steps home.

I remember the first time the dog howled, when a line of firetrucks shrilled up the canyon to try to cut off a brushfire. Puck threw back his head and gave vent to a call so ancient, so lupine really, that it seemed to have more in common with the ravening of fire, the night stalk of predators, than the drowsy life of a house pet. The howl didn't erupt very often, usually kicked off by a siren or a chorus of baying coyotes upcanyon quarreling with the moon. And it was clear Puck didn't like to have us watch him when he did it, especially to laugh or applaud him. He'd been seized by a primal hunger, sacred even, and needed to be alone with it. Usually no more than a minute, and then he'd be back with us, wagging and begging for biscuits.

We didn't have him fixed either. More of an oversight than not, though I wonder now if it didn't have something to do with the neutering Roger and I had been through during our own trapped years in the closet. It meant of course that Puck could be excruciatingly randy. His favorite sexual position was to hump our knees as we lay in bed reading at night, barking insistently if we tried to ignore his throbbing need. We more or less took turns, Roger and I, propping our knees beneath the comforter so Puck could have his ride. He never actually came, not a full load, though he dribbled a lot. I can't say if all this made him more of a gay dog or not.

Except for that nightly erotic charge he never actually jumped up on people, though he could be a handful when friends came over, turning himself inside out to greet them. And for some reason—probably to do with the whole turkey and ham on the buffet—he loved parties, the bigger the better, wagging about from guest to guest all evening, one eye always on the kitchen and the disposition of scraps.

A dog's life, to be sure, but not really a life destined for heroics—huddling beside a wounded hiker to keep him warm or leading smoke-blind tenants from a conflagrated house. That was all right: heroics weren't part of the contract. I read about a woman in England once who applied for a seeing-eye dog but specified that she wanted one who'd flunked. She wasn't *very* blind, you see, and besides she wasn't very good at passing tests herself. So she wanted a sort of second-best companion to muck along with her, doing the best they could. My sentiments exactly. I wasn't planning on any heroics in my life either. Puck didn't have to save me and Roger, and we didn't have to save him.

Except he did save us in the end. I don't see how he could have known about the delirious onset of AIDS, the dread and the fevers, the letting of blood by the bucketful for tests that told us nothing, and finally Roger's exile to UCLA, sentence without parole. I suppose Puck must've picked up on my own panic and grief, suddenly so ignored himself that he probably counted himself lucky to get his supper. I had no expectations of him except that he stay out of the way and have no needs that demanded me. It was then that I began to let him out on his own late at night.

Nobody liked that. Several about-to-be-former friends thought it was terribly irresponsible of me, leaving the dog prey to the coked-out traffic that thundered up the hill when the clubs on the Strip closed. Let alone those coyotes traveling in packs from trash barrel to trash barrel. They didn't understand how rigorously I'd admonish Puck, that he not go far and come back straightaway, any more than they understood they were just displacing the helplessness they felt over Roger's illness. One time Roger's brother had a near foaming tantrum over the sofa in the living room, grimy and doubtless flea-infested from years of dog naps. "You can't expect people to visit," Sheldon sputtered. "It smells like a kennel in here."

No, it actually smelled like death, when you came right down to it. The whole house did. And frankly, the only one who could live with the stink, the battlefield stench of shallow unmarked graves, was Puck. Those who proposed reupholstery as a general solution to keeping death away stopped in less and less, good riddance. The ones who thought we were letting the dog run wild were lucky I didn't sic him on them. Only I really understood, because I saw it happen, how Puck would temper his huge ebullience if Roger was feeling a little fragile. Always there to be petted, sometimes a paw on your knee to nudge you into it.

The world narrowed and narrowed, no end to the tunnel and thus no pin of light in the distance. Not to say there weren't precious months, then weeks, then days, that still had the feel of normalcy. I'd cook up a plate of spaghetti, and we'd sit in the dining room talking of nothing at all, just glad to have a lull in the shelling. And we both looked over one night and saw Puck sitting at attention on his haunches, the sable sheen of his coat set off by the flash of white at his heart, head lifted as if on show, utterly still. In all probability he was just waiting for leftovers. But Roger studied the pose, bemused and quietly beaming with pride, and finally said, "Puck, when did you get to be such a noble beast?"

We both laughed, because we knew we'd had nothing to do with it. But from that point on, Noble Beast became the changeling's nickname. If he took the pose beside you, it meant he wanted his chest scratched. Nothing dramatic, you understand, but somehow Puck came to represent the space left over from AIDS. With no notion of the mortal sting that shaped our human doggedness, he managed to keep the real world ambient, the normal one. Filling it edge to edge with what the thirteenth-century divine, Duns Scotus, called "thisness." There gets to be almost nothing more to say about the daily choke of drugs you have to get down, the nurses streaming in to start the I.V. drips, the numbing reports to the scatter of family and those few friends who've squeaked through with you. Nothing more to say except what the dog brings in, even if it's mostly fleas.

That last morning, when the nurse woke me at seven to say it was very bad, Roger virtually comatose, no time to wait for our noon appointment at UCLA, I leaped out of bed and got us out of there in a matter of minutes. I don't remember the dog underfoot. Only holding Roger upright as we staggered down the steps to the car, talking frantically to keep him conscious. Puck would've been perched on the top step watching us go, he'd done that often enough. But I don't really know what he *saw*, any more than I knew what Roger saw—what dim nimbus of light still lingered after the one eye went blind overnight six months before, the other saved by a thrice-daily blast of acyclovir, but that eye too milked over with a cataract.

He died that night, and the weeks after that are a cataract blur of their own. Somebody must've fed the dog, and I rather have the impression of him wandering among the houseful of family and friends, trying to find someone who'd lead him to Rog. When we brought home from the hospital the last pitiful overnight bag, the final effects as it were, Roger's father shook out the maroon coat sweater and put it on for closeness' sake. And Puck began to leap up and down, dancing about the old man in a circle, barking deliriously. Because he could still smell life in there.

Have we gotten sentimental yet—gone over the edge, as it were? I say there was nothing doing in that first annihilating year of grief, dragging myself out of bed because somebody had to let the dog out, writing so I wouldn't have to think. I can't count the times when I'd crawl under one of the tables where Puck lay sleeping, to hold him so I could cry. He grumbled at being invaded, but his growl was pretty *pro forma*. And somewhere in there I started to talk to him, asking him if he missed Rog, wondering out loud how we were ever going to get through this—daft as a Booth cartoon. He sat unblinking, the Noble Beast as listener.

I don't know when it started, his peculiar habit of barking whenever visitors would leave. I mean, he'd always barked eruptively in greeting, whenever he heard the footfall of a friend coming up the stairs outside. This new bark was something far more urgent, angry and troubled, a peal of warning, so that I'd have to drag him back by the collar as one bewildered friend or another made his drowned-out goodnights. "He doesn't like people to leave," I'd tell them, but still didn't understand for months what he was warning them of: that if they left they might not come back, might get lost the way Roger did. Don't leave, stay here, I'll keep you safe like I keep this man. Meaning me.

Still, he got over the grief sooner than I, testimony to that blessed unconsciousness of death. He became himself again, inexhaustible, excited anew by the dailiness of life. I'm afraid I'd aged much more than he, maybe twenty years for the twenty months of Roger's illness. Puck was still just six, in man-years a warrior still in his prime. I had to do a fair bit of traveling there for a while, the self-appointed seropositive poster child. And Puck would lie waiting under my desk, caretaken by Dan the housesitter, ears perked at every sound outside in case it was I returning from the wars.

Like Argos, Odysseus' dog. Twenty years old and shunted aside because he was too frail to hunt any more. Waiting ten years for his master's return from Troy, and the only one in the palace who recognized the king beneath the grizzle and the tattered raiment. The earliest wagging tail in literature, I believe. No shyness in that time of gods and heroes when it came to the sentiments of reunion, let alone what loyalty meant. So I'd come home from ten days' book-touring, what seemed a mix of

overweening flattery and drive-time call-ins from rabid Baptists
who painted me as the incarnation of Satan. At the end of
which I could scarcely say who the real Monette was, indeed if
there was one at all anymore–till Puck ran out to welcome me.

Around that time I began to feel ready to risk the heart
again, I who hadn't really had a date in fifteen years. I "lingered
hopefully"–to quote the advice that Stevie Smith's lion aunt
read out to her from the lovelorn column, reducing these two
maiden ladies to helpless laughter. Lingered hopefully, I say, at
the edges of various parties, in smoke-filled boites, even at ral-
lies and protests, looking to connect. Held back by my own
sero status as much as anything, unsure if I wanted to find only
another positive, or whether a lucky negative might rescue my
brain from the constant pound of AIDS.

I was sitting on a stationary bike at the gym, pumping hard
and going nowhere, too sweaty to be lingering hopefully. A
young man, thirty or so, came up and stood before me, catch-
ing my eye with a bright expectant nod. "Excuse me," he said,
"but aren't you Edmund White?"

"Not exactly," I retorted. Yet it was such an eccentric pickup
line that I let him pick me up with it. At least he was literate. I
waxed quite eloquent about Ed's work, quite modest about my
own, and gave no thought to the not-so-subtle omen that the
young man might have no interest whatever in Monette, real or
otherwise. After all, if you want to read *Moby Dick, Jane Eyre* just
won't do.

Nevertheless, a few nights later he came over for Chinese
takeout. And took an immediate dislike to Puck–nothing personal, he assured me, all dogs really–but especially not wanting
to sit on the doghaired sofa in his ice-cream linen trousers. Puck
returned the compliment in spades, grumping beneath the coffee table, growling when the young man came too close to me.
I apologized for his ragged manners, then deftly turned the subject to AIDS, my own reality check.

His green eyes lit on me. "There's no reason for anyone to die of that," he observed. "All you have to do is take care of yourself. People who die of it, that's just their excuse."

I left the growling to Puck, too stunned or too Episcopalian to savage my first date since puberty. But I only barely restrained Puck's collar when the young man left, wincing palely at the mastiff shrill of Puck's goodbye.

Stevie had it easier all around. He liked Puck's attitude from the first, a certain orneriness and perversity that neatly matched his own. If you wanted Puck to come over to you, it did no good to call unless you had a biscuit in hand. In fact I had been bribing him so long—a Meaty Bone to get him outside, another to bring him in—he acted as if you must be crazy to order him around without reward. It had to be *his* idea to clamber up on the bed or play with a squeak toy. With the latter he wasn't into give-and-take in any case, but snatched it out of your hand and disappeared with it into his lair. Needless to say, "fetch" wasn't in his vocabulary.

Thus did I learn to back off and feint with Stevie, three months' uncertain courtship. He'd never really made the couple thing work before, and couldn't imagine starting now in the midst of a minefield. Old dog, no new tricks please. It required the barricades for us, going to Washington in October with ACT UP to take over the FDA. A sobbing afternoon spent lurching down the walkways of the quilt, a candle march along the Reflecting Pool with a hundred thousand others. Then massing at FDA headquarters in Maryland, not even dawn yet (and I don't do mornings), standing groggily with Vito Russo as we briefed the press. A standoff most the day, squads of cops huddled as if at a doughnut stand, trying not to arrest us.

And then a small gang of six, all from L.A., found a lacuna in the security. Somebody smashed a ground-floor window, and the L.A. guerrillas poured in—Stevie bringing up the rear, impish as Peter Pan himself. When they dragged him out in handcuffs twenty minutes later, the look that passed between us as they herded him onto a prison van was the purest sign I could've wanted of his being in love with life again. Civil disobedience as an aphrodisiac. Within a day we were lovers for real, unarmed and no turning back.

But he wouldn't move in either, not to my place. I thought it had to do with the freight of memory, too much Roger wherever you looked. But then I understood how determined he was not to turn the house on Kings Road into a sickroom again—a sickroom that only went one way, to the hospice stage and the last racked weeks. From his own falling numbers and all those burials, then the bone-chill sighting of the first lesion on the roof of his mouth, he knew he'd be out of here sooner than I. Unless of course I got hit by the bus that seronegatives were forever invoking to prove we were all a hairsbreadth away from the grave. A bus that was always as far behind schedule as we were ahead of it.

So he began the search for an apartment near me in West Hollywood, but even then we almost broke up a couple of times. He was too far sunk in the quicksand of the endless doctoring, too out of control to be loved. He savaged me one day, calling me blameless even as the arrows found the target of my heart, then fell into a three-day silence. To Victor, who served as go-between in the pained negotiation that followed, he declared: "Why am I breaking up with Paul? I don't know. I like his dog too much."

Oh, that. The fear of getting too attached to the things of life, till you sometimes feel you're better off lying in bed with the shades all down, no visitors welcome. And NO GIFTS, as the invitations all pointedly warn when we agree to a final birthday or one more Christmas. No more things to add to the pile that will only have to be dispersed, the yard sale more certain than heaven or hell.

Happily, Puck and I won out. Steve found a place just

blocks away, a post-mod apartment block behind the Pacific Design Center. And twice a day I'd duck my head under the desk and propose to Puck: "You want to go over to Stevie's?" Then an explosion of barking and dancing, and a long whine of backseat driving as we headed downhill to Huntley Street. As soon as he saw the house Puck would leap from the moving car, to leave his mark on the bushes outside, then bark me into the downstairs garage like some recalcitrant sheep.

Stevie was usually in bed, his I.V's having doubled, or nothing better to do than flip the remote between one numb banality and the next. It gave him a place to center his anger, I think, railing at the bad hair and the laugh tracks. A business where he had once commanded so much power, and now his big-screen set practically needed windshield wipers, there was so much spit expectorated at it.

But his face would brighten like a kid when Puck tore in and bounded on the bed, burrowing in and groaning with pleasure as Stevie gave him a scratch. "Puck, you're better than people," he'd praise the beast—a real irony there, for the beast preferred people to dogs any day.

As for sentiment, Stevie carried that off with the effortless charm that used to be squandered on agents and actors and network VPs. We'd be driving to one of the neighborhood restaurants, pass a street dog rooting for garbage, and Steve would give an appraising look and wonder aloud: "You think he's a friend of Puck's?" No response required from me, as the answer was quickly forthcoming: "I think he is."

In fact, the question went international quite soon thereafter. With so much medicine required on a daily basis, bags of I.V. drugs to be kept chilled, the only way we could travel was by ship. So we cruised through the final year—Monte Carlo to Venice, Tahiti to Bora-Bora, Greece and Turkey—spending the fat disability checks from Columbia. And one day anchored in the Iles des Saintes, blips on the map below Guadalupe, a necklace of pirate lagoons. We motorbiked to the highest point, winding through denuded fields, for goats were the main livestock here.

We sat on a wall of mortared conches and looked out to sea, one of those moments you want to stop time, knowing what torments lie waiting at journey's end. No killer buses in sight right now. From a shack behind us emerged a gaggle of children, and behind them a tiny black goat still wobbly on its kid legs. No way could it keep up with the children running downhill to the harbor. So the goat crossed the road to where we were, made for Stevie and butted his knee, so gently it might have been a kiss. Then did it again. "Friend of Puck's, definitely," Stevie observed with a laugh. A laugh fit for paradise, utterly careless, a holiday from dying.

So what do you carry with you once you have started to leave the world behind? Stevie was right that last Monday in the ICU: he was never going to see Puck again. Didn't even have a chance to say goodbye, except inside. For his part Puck made his own bewildered peace, still tearing into Huntley Street as we packed and gave away one man's universe of things, the beast still hoping against hope that Stevie himself would walk in any minute.

I understand that a housedog is yet another ridiculous privilege of having means in a world gone mad with suffering. I've seen the scrawny dogs that follow refugees around, war after pointless war. The dogs have long disappeared from the starvation camps of Somalia, long since eaten, the dogless camps of Laos and Bangladesh. There is nothing to pet in the end. Perhaps it is worse than sentimental, the direst form of denial, to still be weeping at dog stories. But I admit it. Puck has gone gray in the face now, stiff in the legs when he stands, and I am drawn to stories about dogs who visit nursing homes and hospitals, unafraid of frailty and the nearness of death. Dogs, in a word, who don't flunk.

And I weep these incorrigible tears. Two years ago I was in a posh photo gallery in New York with a friend, and we asked to see the Wegmans. I maintained a rigorous connoisseur's posture, keeping it all high-toned, for there were those who were very suspicious of the popularity of Man Ray, the supreme model of Wegman's canine fantasias. A general wariness that Wegman's audience might be more interested in dogs than art. In my case doubly so, since to me at least Puck could have been Man Ray's twin. Same color, same shape, same humanness.

Now of course Man Ray was gone, and though he'd been replaced in the studio by the sleek and estimable Fay, no mean model herself, prices for a vintage Man had gone through the roof. Anyway, this curatorial assistant, very Fifty-seventh Street, brought out of a drawer with white gloves three big Polaroids of Man, maybe 30-by-40 inches apiece. In one the dog was stretched on his back with his paws up, no gimmicks and costume accessories here, just a dog at rest. You could tell he was old from the shiver of gray on his snout. I found it so unbearably moving I choked on tears and could not look at another.

So after Stevie was buried, I figured Puck and I were set for twilight, seven years for every twelvemonth, a tossup still as to who'd go first. We didn't plan on letting anyone else in. Not depressed or even defeated yet—just exhausted, the heart brimful already with seized days and a sort of Homeric loyalty. We shared a wordless language and had no expectations. Like the old man and his dog in De Sica's masterpiece *Umberto D*, who cannot save each other but can't leave either. They'd rather starve together.

Then I met Winston. It was a bare two months since Steve had died, and Victor and I had just returned from three weeks' melancholy touring in Europe, weeping in cathedrals so to speak. I recall telling Victor on the flight home that I could probably still connect with someone, but only if that someone could handle the steamship load of AIDS baggage I carried with me. Somehow Winston could juggle it with his own, or at least the risk and intoxication of love made even the dead in our arms lighter. By Christmas we were lovers, and Puck couldn't help but give us his blessing, so showered was he by Winston with rubber bones and yank toys: "This dog has got nothing to play with!"

This dog was not the only one. And because there is never enough time anymore, by mid-January we were deep into the chess match of Winston's move into Kings Road. Just one small problem, really—a four-year-old boxer called Buddy. He'd grown up on a ranch, free to run and in titular charge of a barnful of horses and a tribe of cats. The first meeting of our two unfixed males wasn't promising in the least. Buddy jumped on Puck right off, sending the two of them into a whirlwind ball of snarling and gnashing, leaving Winston and me no choice but to wade in after and pull them apart. Buddy was clearly the aggressor here, but then we were on his territory.

The situation didn't improve when Buddy came to stay at Kings Road. Puck simply couldn't believe it that his slumbering twilight had thus been invaded. He stuck to his lairs and growled with ferocious menace if Buddy came anywhere near. In fact, if we weren't absolutely vigilant we had a sudden dogfight on our hands. There was nothing for it but to separate them at opposite ends of the house, the doors all closed. It was like a French farce, the constant flinging and slamming of doors, enough entrances and exits to rival the court of the Louis.

You get used to accommodations when everyone you know is dying. It was clear that Buddy was a pussycat at heart—despite my childhood terror of a boxer named Sergeant, a neighborhood ruffian known for snapping at kids and rumored to have devoured whole several meek suburban lapdogs who happened to look at him funny. Buddy's gentle spirit was every bit as benign as Puck's lab side, except when they were together. And

Buddy was meticulously trained as well, as rigorous as a Balanchine dancer, responding with infinite grace to all of his master's commands. Responding to food alone, Puck didn't know quite what to make of the military precision of his housemate.

Puck was fed on the front porch, Buddy in the back yard. It was no more peculiar in its way than families who can't stand each other, sitting silent at the dinner table, invisible lines drawn. If Winston and I hadn't been able to laugh about it, I'm not sure it could have gone on so long. By April he had bit the bullet and gotten Buddy fixed, though we were warned it could take six months for the pugnacity around Puck to abate. Puck's balls followed on the chopping block in June, since his Arab/Indian vet reassured me Puck would have less problems aging, less chance of tumors if he was fixed.

They didn't really seem any different that summer, except that Puck wouldn't hump our knees with the same rollicking passion. He humped all right, but it seemed to be more of an afterthought, a memory trace, over in a matter of seconds. I didn't have much leisure to notice, frankly, with my own numbers falling precipitously and three ribs broken from taking a dive off a trotting horse. The walls of AIDS were closing in, no matter how many names I dropped, or how tortuous my progress through the drug underground, scoring the latest miracle. It was all I could do not to drown in my own panic, or take it out on Winston. My attitude towards the dogs was more implicit than not, but Puck had been there before. There were times when dogs just had to be dogs—no neediness, please, and no misbehaving. The merest tick became a problem I couldn't handle.

By the end of summer I'd started to run daily fevers—99.5 at five P.M., like clockwork. My numbers continued to tumble, under a hundred now. Winston had to fly up to Seattle over Labor Day weekend to visit his former lover John, who'd taken a very bad turn. It was the first time I'd had care of the two dogs by myself. All I really wanted to do was sit at the word processor, three or four pages to go in *Becoming a Man*. And it seemed I spent all day opening and closing doors, a farce for solo performer.

Finally I'd had it. I called Buddy in from the bedroom, Puck from the fleabag sofa. I sat them down at opposite ends of the study, threatening them direly if they dared make a move towards each other. They both blinked at me as I lectured them: this separate-but-equal shit had got to stop. "Now lie down and be good boys," I announced with a final flourish. And they did. Puzzled, to be sure, by the heat of my remarks, not having been seized by the door issue with quite my sense of drama.

There were still rough edges, of course. Now that they managed to be together without attacking, they began to steal toys from one another, swooping in and snatching, the growls just short of a major explosion. The problem was, Puck didn't know how to play—as loath to share as a bully in the kindergarten. The toys would pile up in his lair, guarded like meat, the spoiled brat who takes his baseball home so nobody else can enjoy. Buddy—such a prince—was the one who was eager to play in earnest, and yet he'd yield to Puck and forego the tearing around the house for which he had energy to burn. More to the point, Buddy abdicated his male position of dominance—turning the other cheek, so to speak, rather than bristling. It may have been the loss of balls that let it happen, but clearly Buddy preferred to have a friend than to be on top.

Gradually Puck learned to give a little back, permitting Buddy to do his racing about with a mauled stuffed Dumbo in his mouth, while Puck stood ground and barked. In fact, if Buddy gets credit for teaching Puck the rudiments of play, the pedagogy went the other way when it came to making noise. When Buddy first arrived he didn't make a peep, never having been needed somehow as a watchdog at the ranch. Thus he'd watch with a certain fascination as Puck, alert to every sound outside, especially the arrival of delivery men, would run to the front door bellowing doom. It took a fair amount of time for Buddy to get the hang of it—a softer bark in any case, here too letting Puck be the lead singer—but now they both leap up clamoring, barreling by one another as they scramble to investigate.

Yet it's Puck who's had to yield in the barking department, sharing the bellow and guard duties. After all, Buddy's hearing is finer, his high-pointed ears like radar. Puck's has dimmed by contrast in his twelfth year, so he doesn't quite catch as quick as he used to the slam of every car door. More often now Buddy's the one who pricks to the sound of something out there, the first to woof, so that Puck's scramble to join the fray is an act of following.

And Puck has been more than a little grateful to turn the rat chores over to Buddy. Brown field rats, not so horrible as the gray vermin that haunt the docks and garbage dumps of the world. Sometimes one gets in because the kitchen door is open to the back yard, to give the dogs easy access. It's happened a couple of times that Puck and I have surprised a rodent in the kitchen, and I shriek and Puck barks, and somehow the freaked-out rat scoots out.

But Buddy's a ratter. He sniffs them out and waits for them to make a move from under the stove or the washing machine. He'll wait for hours if necessary. And then the rodent makes a dash for the kitchen door, and Buddy's on him—unafraid to clamp his jaws around the squirming intruder and give him a bad shake. He doesn't kill them, just scares the bejesus out of them. If I were a rat I would not be coming back soon. And since I can't stand to trap them any more—that awful springing snap as the tri-arm breaks their leg or their neck—I much prefer the Buddy method of pest control.

It would be too simple to call them brothers now, too anthropomorphic by half. Each has retained the marks and idiosyncracies of his breed quite distinctly. Buddy is what is called a "flashy fawn," because all four paws are white as well as his breastplate, and a marvelous free-form zigzag just behind the ears. He can't stand getting wet, doesn't even like to be in the back garden after it's been watered, practically walking on tiptoe. While Puck no longer dives in the pool like he used to, swimming laps with Roger, water is still his element. On a very hot day he'll still step down in and dog-paddle in a tight circle to cool off.

Not brothers then, but comrades. Like any other dogs they sleep more than anything else, but sometimes now they do it flank to flank, almost curled about each other. When they sit on their haunches side by side in the kitchen doorway, lingering hopefully for biscuits, they are most definitely a pair. Puck taught Buddy to beg by the way, a serious breach in his training. When they go outside together, however, Buddy knows he can go no further than the edge of the terrace, not down the steps. Puck on the other hand sprawls himself on the landing at the top of the stairs, one step down from the terrace, his life-long perch for overseeing the neighborhood. Thus Buddy stands above Puck, though one would be hard put to say who's taking care of whom.

That they look after each other is clear. It's an act of faith among zoologists that there's no homosex in the animal world. Gay is a human orientation, period. But just as I've come to understand, late in my own dog years, that being gay is a matter of identity much larger than carnality, I don't think the mating instinct is all the story. What the two dogs have with one another is an easy sort of intimacy, the opposite of straight men. Thus they sniff each other's butthole as casually as men shake hands. Not gay then, exactly, even though both have grown up surrounded by a tribe of us. Call them different, that comes closest. As if being together has changed them so, they've become more than themselves—a continuum of eccentricities traded off and mimicked, grounded by their willingness to be tamed, loyal before all else. Not unlike Winston and me, and we're as gay as they come.

Meanwhile, twilight deepens. The dogs whoop with delight when Ande the nurse comes to call, once a week these days so I can get my I.V. dose of Amphotericin. They do not see her as a chill reminder of my sickness, any more than I do. We sustain this life as best we can, propelled by the positive brand of denial, the nearest approximation we can make to the bliss of dogs and their mortal ignorance. Thus I can watch Puck age and feel it tear at me, while he can't watch me dwindle or even see the lesions. Somehow it makes him wiser than I, for all my overstuffed brains, book-riddled and smart to a fault.

We go along like we always have, a houseful of four instead of two. Every few weeks Puck and I cross Kings Road to visit Mrs. Knecht, our neighbor lady who lost her husband in '85 to a sudden heart attack. She endures in her eighties, a tribute to her Austrian stalwartness, her family wiped out in the camps. Assaulted by the indignities of age, Mrs. Knecht doesn't have a lot of pleasures anymore, but Puck is one. I'm terrified that he'll knock her down when he barrels into her house, that he'll take her hand off when she feeds him biscuits. But that is what she likes best about him, I think, his indomitable eagerness, his stallion force. Mrs. Knecht is our good deed, Puck's and mine, but also serving to remind all three of us that life goes on among the loyal.

Nights we stay up later than Buddy and Winston, a couple of hours at least. Buddy's curled in his basket under the bedroom window, and Winston like Roger sleeps without pills, deeper than I ever get. Yet I can't really say that Puck stays up with me as I potter around in the still of the night. He sleeps then too, though always near me, and would call it keeping me company if he had words. All he knows is, nothing is likely at this hour to bother us or require our vigilance. It will go on like this forever, as far as Puck can see. For his sake then I try to see no further, relishing these hours out of time.

It has already been decided: if I go first Winston has promised to care for him, to keep what's left of the family together. If Puck goes first, a painless shot to ease some awful arthritic misery and send him to sleep, I promise nothing. The vets will tell you, there are suicides in the parking lot after the putting down of pets. For some it's the last last straw.

But for tonight I'm glad we have endured together and, as they say in the romance genre, lived to love again. We will not be returning from Troy, either of us, but meanwhile we are one another's anchor to the best of the past, a matter of trust and bondedness that goes all the way back to prehistory. One of us is descended from wolves; one of us knows he's dying. Together we somehow have the strength to bear it, tonight at least, when the moon is down and no creature howls. What we dream is exactly the same, of course, that nothing will change.

At two A.M. he whimpers at the door to go out, and I let him go. Usually he's back in half an hour, but you never know what will take him further, what trail will beckon him up through the chaparral. He knows me too well. That I'll wait up all night if necessary till he comes panting home. That even if I rail at him like a crabby parent in curlers, he'll still get a biscuit before the lights go out. Because all that matters to either of us is that the other one's still here—fellow survivors of so much breakage to the heart, not a clue when the final siren will sound. But guarding the world for dear life anyway, even as it goes. Noble beast.

ACKNOWLEDGMENTS

We wish to thank the following authors, literary agents, publishers, and organizations for permission to publish or reprint the pieces in this book.

ANONYMOUS: "One Mother's Story," copyright © 1995 by M.O. Published by arrangement with the author. All rights reserved.

ANONYMOUS: "Unsafe Sex," copyright ©1995 by C.T. Published by arrangement with the author. All rights reserved.

CHRISTINE BOOSE: "Fear of AIDS Killed Sarah," from *New Youth Connections*, copyright ©1990 by Youth Communication. Reprinted by permission of Youth Communication, New York Center, Inc.

HAROLD BRODKEY: "To My Readers," copyright ©1993 by Harold Brodkey, reprinted with the permission of Wylie, Aitken & Stone, Inc. First published in *The New Yorker*.

RAFAEL CAMPO: "AIDS and the Poetry of Healing," copyright © 1993 by Rafael Campo. First published in *The Kenyon Review*, Fall 1993. Reprinted by permission of the author.

JOSHUA CLOVER: "Letter from Stephen," copyright © 1995 by Joshua Clover. First published in *In the Company of My Solitude*, by arrangement with the author.

218 ·

IRIS DE LA CRUZ: "Sex, Drugs, Rock-n-Roll, and AIDS," from *Women, AIDS & Activism* by the ACT UP/NY Women & AIDS Book Group, copyright © 1990, 1992 by the ACT UP/New York Women and AIDS Book Group. Reprinted by permission of South End Press.

TORY DENT: "Loose Rider" by Tory Dent, copyright © 1995 by Tory Dent, from a work-in-progress. All rights reserved. Published by permission of the author.

MARK DOTY: "Is There a Future?" copyright 1995 by Mark Doty. First published in *In the Company of My Solitude*, by arrangement with the author.

MELVIN DIXON: "I'll Be Somewhere Listening for My Name," copyright © 1992 by Melvin Dixon. Excerpted from keynote address at OutWrite 92: The Third National Lesbian and Gay Writers Conference, Boston, Massachusetts. Reprinted by permission of Faith Childs Literary Agency and the Estate of Melvin Dixon.

CAROL MUSKE DUKES: "All Through the Night," copyright © 1995 by Carol Muske Dukes. First published in *In the Company of My Solitude*, by arrangement with the author.

EVE ENSLER: "All of Us Are Leaving," copyright © 1993 by Eve Ensler. First published in *In the Company of My Solitude*, by arrangement with the author.

PATRICK HOCTEL: "A Beautiful Day in the Week," copyright © 1995 by Patrick D. Hoctel. First published in *In the Company of My Solitude*, by arrangement with the author.

FENTON JOHNSON: "Lucky Fellow" copyright © 1993 by Fenton Johnson and "The Limitless Heart," copyright © 1991 by Fenton Johnson. Both first published in *The New York Times Magazine*. Reprinted by permission of the author.

JAMES LECESNE: "Now Is the Time for All Good," copyright © 1995 by James Lecesne. First published in *In the Company of My Solitude*, by arrangement with the author.

ROBERT MASSA: "Specimen Days," copyright © 1994 by Robert Massa. First published in *The Village Voice*. Reprinted by permission of the Estate of Robert Massa and *The Village Voice*.

MARK MATOUSEK: "Savage Grace," copyright © 1993, 1995 by Mark Matousek. First published in somewhat different form in *Common Boundary*. Reprinted by permission of the author.

RICHARD MCCANN: "Pornography," copyright © 1994 by Richard McCann. Reprinted by arrangement with the author and Brandt and Brandt, Inc.

PAUL MONETTE: "Puck," copyright © 1993 by Paul Monette. Also collected in *Last Watch of the Night* by Paul Monette. Reprinted by permission of the author.

MARY JANE NEALON: "Realizations at Bedside," copyright © 1992, 1995 by Mary Jane Nealon. Published in a different form in *Buying America Back*, edited by William Kistler and Jonathan Greenberg (Council Oak Publishing Co. Inc., Tulsa, Oklahoma). Reprinted by arrangement with the author.

FRAN PEAVEY: "A Shallow Pool of Time," is excerpted from *A Shallow Pool of Time* by Fran Peavey, copyright © 1990 by Crabgrass Foundation. Reprinted by permission of New Society Publishers, 4527 Springfield Avenue, Philadelphia, Pennsylvania 19143.

TOM PHILLIPS: "Jimmy Parker" and "Jean LeChance," copyright © 1995 by Tom Phillips. First published in *In the Company of My Solitude*, by arrangement with the author.

DENISE RIBBLE: "A Day in the Life," from *AIDS: The Women,* edited by Ines Rieder and Patricia Ruppelt, copyright © 1988 by Ines Rieder and Patricia Ruppelt. Reprinted by permission of Cleis Press.

MARLON RIGGS: "Letters to the Dead," copyright © 1993 by Marlon T. Riggs. Reprinted by permission of the Estate of Marlon T. Riggs.

DEBORAH SALAZAR: "The Bad News Is the Bad News Is the Same," copyright © 1994 by Deborah Salazar. Reprinted by permission of *Exquisite Corpse* and the author.

KATE SCANNELL: "Skills and Pills," from *AIDS: The Women,* edited by Ines Rieder and Patricia Ruppelt, copyright © 1988 by Ines Rieder and Patricia Ruppelt. Reprinted by permission of Cleis Press.

ANDREW SULLIVAN: "Quilt," copyright © 1992 by The New Republic, Inc. Reprinted by permission of *The New Republic.*

AKIA THOMAS: "My Favorite Uncle Is HIV-Positive," from *New Youth Connections,* copyright © 1994 by Youth Communication. Reprinted by permission of Youth Communication, New York Center, Inc.

A NOTE ABOUT
THE EDITORS

———————————— · ————————————

MARIE HOWE is the author of a book of poems, *The Good Thief,* which was a selection in the National Poetry Series. Her second volume is entitled *What the Living Do.* Howe teaches graduate writing students at Sarah Lawrence College and at the Warren Wilson Program for Writers.

MICHAEL KLEIN teaches at Sarah Lawrence College and in the MFA Program at Goddard College. His two previous books, *Poets for Life: 76 Poets Respond to AIDS* (which he edited) and *1990* (a book of poems) won Lambda Literary Awards in 1989 and 1993 respectively. He is currently performing a one-man show called *10,000 Hands Have Touched Me,* which is also the title of his latest book.